D1534925

THE DIVINE APOSTLE

THE
DIVINE APOSTLE

THE INTERPRETATION OF
ST PAUL'S EPISTLES IN THE
EARLY CHURCH

BY

MAURICE F. WILES

Dean of Clare College in the University of Cambridge

CAMBRIDGE
AT THE UNIVERSITY PRESS
1967

Published by the Syndics of the Cambridge University Press
Bentley House, 200 Euston Road, London, N.W.1
American Branch: 32 East 57th Street, New York, N.Y. 10022

Library of Congress Catalogue Card Number: 67–13809

Printed in Great Britain
at the University Printing House, Cambridge
(Brooke Crutchley, University Printer)

CONTENTS

ABBREVIATIONS

The following standard abbreviations have been used.

E.T. English Translation

G.C.S. *Die Griechischen Christlichen Schriftsteller der ersten drei Jahrhunderte*

H.E. *Historia Ecclesiastica*

H.T.R. *Harvard Theological Review*

J.B.L. *Journal of Biblical Literature*

J.T.S. *Journal of Theological Studies*

P.G. *Patrologia Graeca, Cursus Completus*, ed. J.-P. Migne

P.L. *Patrologia Latina, Cursus Completus*, ed. J.-P. Migne

Z.N.W. *Zeitschrift für Neutestamentliche Wissenschaft*

Z.R.G. *Zeitschrift für Religions- und Geistesgeschichte*

INTRODUCTION

In my earlier book *The Spiritual Gospel* I set out to study the way in which St John's Gospel was interpreted by the early Greek commentators. In *The Divine Apostle* I have attempted a similar study with respect to the letters of St Paul. This task has proved for a number of reasons a more difficult one to handle. In the first place St John's Gospel is a single work whereas St Paul wrote many letters. I have excluded Hebrews and the Pastoral epistles from my survey even though they were generally regarded by the Fathers as Pauline, but we are still left with ten letters of very varied character. Secondly, the volume of patristic commentary is both greater in quantity and also more variegated and more fragmentary in character. In particular we have a far wider range of Latin commentaries than in the case of St John's Gospel and it has seemed right to bring these also within the scope of the inquiry. Thirdly, although St John's Gospel was more central to the main development of Christological doctrine than St Paul's writings, yet the range of doctrinal issues raised in any attempt to expound St Paul was probably even wider than in the case of St John. A comprehensive treatment of all the issues which arise in the course of reading the patristic exegesis of St Paul's writings would require a complete history of early doctrinal development. The scope of this work is a much more limited one. In the first place I have drawn for the most part only upon the actual commentaries; my aim in so doing has been to try to show how certain important aspects of Pauline thought were understood and interpreted by early scholars engaged directly upon the work of commentary and exegesis. At times, however, in order to present as clearly as possible the developing pattern of ideas, it has been necessary to go outside the actual commentaries themselves; where I have done so, I have always attempted to concentrate attention upon the extent to which and the manner in which those developing ideas were consciously based upon Pauline teaching. In such cases I have indicated in the notes not only the relevant patristic texts but also the particular scriptural texts on which the patristic argument was explicitly based. Secondly, my purpose is essentially historical in character. In other words my fundamental aim has been simply to trace out the main ways in which St Paul's writings were expounded in the early centuries. I have ventured from time to time, especially in the final assessment, to suggest reasons which may help to explain this course of development and to give some indication of its worth. But my main purpose is descriptive rather than evaluative. I have not attempted to adjudge in detail just how far the early commentators were or were not correct in their understanding of St Paul. Such judgements could only be made on the basis of an agreed understanding of St Paul which, within the range of such a book as this, would have to be assumed rather than argued. In recent studies of the patristic exegesis of St Paul, which have attempted to present their material throughout in terms of such evaluative judgements, it is my not infrequent experience to find that any points of disagreement with them arise more often from differences in the understanding of St Paul's thought (which in the particular work has been largely assumed) than from differences in the understanding of the Fathers (which is the more direct and detailed subject of the study).[1] I have therefore made it my goal here simply to set out as carefully as I can how the Fathers in fact interpreted St Paul. Whoever is confident that he knows the true exegesis of St Paul's thought will then be in a position to answer for himself the question how far the interpretation given by the Fathers is correct.

[1] E.g. F. Buri, *Clemens Alexandrinus und der Paulinische Freiheitsbegriff*; U. Wickert, *Studien zu den Pauluskommentaren Theodors von Mopsuestia*.

CHAPTER I

THE COMMENTATORS

The incorporation of a group of letters within the fold of Holy Scripture is one of the more striking features of the Christian canon. The story of how this came about is still a subject of debate, and unfortunately our evidence is so slender that at present it must remain largely a matter for conjecture. At least the process seems to have been virtually complete before the end of the second century, so that for all Christian writers from that time on there existed a corpus of Pauline letters which were regarded as having the status and authority of Scripture. Whatever it was that prompted the early Church to promote Paul's writings to this exalted status, it was not the simplicity or clarity of their message. II Peter iii. 16 bears testimony to the co-existence of a deep respect for the profundity and wisdom of Paul's letters with a recognition of their difficulty and of the possibility of their serious misinterpretation. It has been the frequent contention of Protestant scholars that this misinterpretation of Paul's thought within the early Church was by no means restricted to those heretical circles which the author of II Peter had in mind. Rather it is to be seen present, albeit unconsciously present, in the most orthodox and fervent admirers of Paul. Harnack's dictum that the second-century Fathers completely failed to understand Paul apart from Marcion, who misunderstood him, has become proverbial. E. Hoffman-Aleith concludes a study of Chrysostom's interpretation of Paul by declaring that he is a striking example of how the theologians of the early Church combined an admiration for Paul with an unconscious failure to understand him.[1] Many similar examples could be quoted. But this is not the only kind of judgement that has been passed. Roman Catholic scholars in particular have been inclined to give a very different verdict. Lagrange, for example, speaks of Chrysostom's homilies on Romans as 'un commentaire perpétuel, le plus beau que nous ait

---

[1] 'Das Paulusverständnis des Johannes Chrysostomus', *Z.N.W.* xxxviii (1939), 188.

laissé l'antiquité' and says of his commentary on Galatians that it is Chrysostom 'qui reflète le mieux la pensée chrétienne et l'âme de Paul'.[1] The majority of scholars no doubt would steer a course somewhat between these two extremes,[2] but an immense range of differing judgement remains. Any sifting of the elements of truth and untruth in such conflicting claims can only be made in the light of a careful analysis of the work of the early commentators. It is the aim of this study to provide such an analysis. But first of all we must review briefly who those early commentators were, what works of theirs have come down to us and in what circumstances they were written.[3]

Paul's writings are quoted as authoritative Christian writings from a very early stage. The first half of the second century is a period from which very little Christian literature has come down to us. Polycarp of Smyrna is as representative a figure of the main stream of Christian life and thought during that period as it would be possible to name. In his epistle to the Philippians (probably about A.D. 135) he quotes Eph. iv. 26 alongside a quotation from the Old Testament as 'Scriptura'.[4] The Gnostic Basilides was a man of very different ideas but of very similar date; he is reported as having quoted I Cor. ii. 13 as ἡ γραφή.[5] Later in the century we find Irenaeus citing the words of Gal. v. 21 with a similar introductory phrase.[6] The word γραφή at that stage had admittedly a rather wider connotation than would be implied by the

---

[1] M. J. Lagrange, *Épître aux Romains* viii; *Épître aux Galates* viii (quoted by A. Merzagora, 'Giovanni Crisostomo, Commentatore di S. Paolo', *Didaskaleion*, n.s. x (1931), 5). Merzagora (*art. cit.* p. 1) also quotes the famous saying of Isidore (*Epp.* 5, 32), with special reference to the commentary on Romans, that if Paul had known Attic Greek he would have interpreted himself in precisely the way in which Chrysostom in fact did. Cf. also B. Altaner, *Patrologie*, p. 291 (E.T. pp. 378–9).

[2] E.g. H. E. W. Turner, *The Pattern of Christian Truth* (1954), p. 485; K. H. Schelkle, *Paulus Lehrer der Väter* (1936), p. 440.

[3] For more detailed information on the commentaries themselves, see in the case of the Greek commentaries C. H. Turner, 'Greek Patristic Commentaries on the Pauline Epistles', in the extra volume of Hastings, *Dictionary of the Bible*, and in the case of the Latin commentaries, A. Souter, *The Earliest Latin Commentaries on the Epistles of St Paul* (1927).

[4] Epistle of Polycarp, 12.

[5] Hippolytus, *Elenchos*, 7, 26, 3.

[6] Irenaeus, *Adv. Haer.* 1, 6, 3 (Harvey, 1, 55).

English word 'Scripture'.[1] Nevertheless, we may safely assert that by the close of the second century the letters of Paul had established themselves in the eyes of the Church as authoritative Scripture alongside the Old Testament and the Gospels. Such groups as the Ebionites might indeed refuse to accept them, but that was only evidence of their heretical or even fundamentally unchristian character.[2] No doubt the division between those who accepted and those who rejected Paul's writings was not always clear-cut. Some, like Tatian, rejected 'some epistles of Paul' although in practice drawing upon his writings in the exposition of their own teaching.[3] But all such exceptions were of comparatively limited extent and of only temporary significance. Throughout the second century the great majority of Christians and would-be Christians were concerned to find in Paul's writings support for their particular understanding of Christian truth. And from the beginning of the third century onwards the canonization in practice of those writings was more or less complete and any statement of the Christian case had to be based upon them as surely as it had to be based upon the Old Testament and the Gospels. Thus the beginning of the third century represents approximately the stage at which Paul's letters had reached a sufficiently fixed and exalted status in the eyes of the Church for the work of systematic commentary to begin.

Nevertheless, the nature of the appeal to Paul in the second century is not without significance, for it provides the background of thought which in part called out the earliest works of commentary and in no small measure determined their character. Marcion's special dependence on the Pauline writings is well known, and more will be said of it when we come to deal with the interpretation of Paul's teaching about the law.[4] But the other great second-century Gnostics, such as Valentinus and Basilides, also drew upon his letters. In particular they found there valuable evidence for their ideas about

[1] Cf. J. Werner, *Der Paulinismus des Irenaeus* (1889), pp. 35–46; J. Lawson, *Biblical Theology of St Irenaeus* (1948), p. 51.

[2] Irenaeus, *Adv. Haer.* 1, 26, 2 (Harvey, 1, 212–13); Origen, *Con. Cel.* 5, 65; *Hom. in Jer.* 19, 12.

[3] Jerome, *Comm. in Tit.* Prolog. (556A). See R. M. Grant, 'Tatian and the Bible', *Studia Patristica*, 1, 300–3.

[4] See chapter IV below.

the nature of man and esoteric knowledge.[1] This tradition of interpretation was well known to the great Alexandrian scholars, Clement and Origen, who are the first Pauline commentators known to us. The refutation of Gnostic claims was never far from their minds as they came to give their own exegesis of Paul's meaning.

Of Clement little can be said. We know that he commented very briefly on all the epistles in his lost work, the *Hypotyposes*,[2] but only a very few excerpts have survived through quotation in later writings. His comments appear to have amounted to little more than very short notes, and it is rather with Origen that the real work of exegetical commentary begins. Origen's productivity was enormous. Best known to us for his commentaries and homilies on the Old Testament and the Gospels, he seems also to have written commentaries on all the Pauline epistles. These were not planned as a single continuous commentary, and indeed varied considerably in their length and thoroughness of treatment. All seem to have belonged to his Caesarean rather than his Alexandrian period. But of this vast output only a fraction remains. Interesting fragments survive from the commentaries on I Corinthians and on Ephesians, but the only one to survive in any substantial form is that on Romans. This exists in an abridged Latin translation by Rufinus. Among the papyri discovered at Tura in 1941 was a much longer section of the original Greek text than had previously been available, and this has enabled some check to be made on the reliability of Rufinus' translation. The resulting judgement has proved on the whole to be a vindication of Rufinus,[3] and it seems permissible therefore to use Rufinus' version with a fair measure of confidence except when the translator's hand is clearly evident.

The survival of the commentary on Romans and the decision that the translation of Rufinus is in general a reliable guide to Origen's exegesis are matters of no small importance for our study. For Origen stands out in splendid isolation at the fountain-head of the tradition of Greek exegesis. We do not even know of the existence of any other

[1] Irenaeus, *Adv. Haer.* 1, 8, 3 (Harvey, 1, 72) (I Cor. ii. 14–15; xv. 48); Hippolytus, *Elenchos*, 7, 26, 3 (I Cor. ii. 13). See chapter III below.

[2] Eusebius, *H.E.* 6, 14, 1; Photius, *Bibl. Cod.* 109 (*P.G.* 103, 381 D–384 A).

[3] See H. Chadwick, 'Rufinus and the Tura Papyrus of Origen's Commentary on Romans', *J.T.S.* n.s. x.

commentaries from the third century. The next surviving Greek commentaries are a full century and a half after his time. They belong to the years surrounding the start of the fifth century and are the work of the two great Antiochenes, John Chrysostom and Theodore of Mopsuestia.

From the pen of Chrysostom we have writings on every one of Paul's letters. In the case of the Epistle to the Galatians the work is in the form of a commentary; all the rest are treated in homilies. The majority of these were delivered at Antioch, and therefore before A.D. 397, though a few, notably the homilies on Colossians, belong to his Constantinopolitan period. Despite the essentially homiletic purpose of the writings, Chrysostom does enter with comparative thoroughness into detailed questions of the correct exegesis of the text. It may be indeed that the homiletic method has some advantages in the treatment of letters, whose original purpose was certainly nearer to that of homiletic than to that of theological definition.

Theodore of Mopsuestia was Chrysostom's fellow-student in the school of Diodore at Antioch. Theodore's work took the form not of sermons but of commentaries on all the Pauline epistles. The Church of the sixth century regarded him as a precursor of Nestorius, and both he and his writings were condemned at the Council of Constantinople in A.D. 553. As a consequence hardly any of his original writings have survived and, as with Origen, we are dependent either on fragments or on translations. Of his commentaries on Romans and the two Corinthian epistles only fragments remain, but we are fortunate to possess a full and substantially reliable Latin translation of his commentaries on all Paul's other epistles. The commentaries are to be dated in the later period of Theodore's life and belong to the early years of the fifth century. They are works of outstanding interest and remarkable exegetical insight, which help to show why Theodore should have earned in his own day the nickname of 'the Interpreter'.

The century and a half which separates Chrysostom and Theodore from Origen was a period of vigorous theological debate. The Eastern Church was divided during much of the period not only by ecclesiastical rivalries but by genuine differences in the understanding of the faith. The controversies associated with the names of Arius and Apollinarius may have been bedevilled by many extraneous non-theological factors, but they did involve a serious grappling with the theological meaning of the Scriptures. The absence of any surviving commentaries on the Pauline epistles from the period does not mean that no commentaries were written. It was in fact a period of great activity in the writing of commentaries. The work of biblical exegesis could contribute both to the building up of the faithful (for even though the period may impinge upon us primarily as a period of councils, creeds and controversies, the essential day-to-day life of the Church was being carried on all the time with vigour and devotion) and also at the same time to the exposition and defence of theological conviction. For importance in this latter respect the Pauline epistles were second only to St John's Gospel.

Our knowledge of the work done during the period derives from the fragments preserved in the catenae or chain-commentaries of later centuries. In the later patristic age the main emphasis in scholarship was not on new creation but on the preservation of the old. Men were content to produce commentaries on the books of Scripture in the form of a chain of extracts from the work of earlier exegetes without expressing any judgement or conclusions of their own. It is to this traditionalist spirit that we owe such limited knowledge as we have of Greek exegetical writing on the Pauline epistles between the times of Origen and Chrysostom. Moreover, these later catenists seem to have been unusually free from dogmatic bias; they were prepared to record comments which seemed to them to be of exegetical worth even though they came from the pen of authors generally regarded as heretical. Our knowledge of the exegetical tradition of the period, therefore, though very limited, is representative of a wider range of theological opinion than might have been expected. It has, however, always been necessary to exercise great care in making use of these catenae, because the extracts are not always assigned clearly or accurately to their proper authors. But the catena fragments on the Pauline epistles have been excellently edited by K. Staab in his *Pauluskommentare aus der griechischen Kirche*. They contain no extracts from the third century nor even from the earliest years of the fourth. But from the middle years of the fourth century we have fragments of Eusebius of Emesa on Galatians and Acacius of Caesarea on Romans. Doctrinally both belonged to the group usually described as semi-Arian, and may serve as important reminders that the anti-Arians had no monopoly of sound scholarship at that time. Indeed it is probable that the best and fullest work of commentary on the Pauline epistles after the time of Origen was the work of another mid-fourth-century writer of the same general theological persuasion, Theodore of Heraclea; but in his case not even fragments have survived. Further fragments from commentaries on Romans survive from the hands of Diodore and Apollinarius. Both were vigorous opponents of Arianism, though themselves in direct conflict with one another on the question of Christological belief. Both stood in the Antiochene tradition in matters of exegesis, and their real importance cannot be measured by the paucity of the surviving fragments. Diodore was undoubtedly a paramount influence on the thought both of Chrysostom and of Theodore: Apollinarius, in spite of his heresy, was still regarded by Jerome as being (together with Didymus the Blind) second only in importance to Origen as a source to be consulted in the work of Pauline exegesis. From within the Alexandrian tradition we have slightly more extended fragments on Romans and the two Corinthian epistles from Didymus and Cyril of Alexandria, but in their cases also the total volume is only small. The one writer of the period who is extensively represented in the catenae with comments on all the epistles is Severian of Gabala. He was a jealous rival and bitter opponent of Chrysostom in the unhappy days of his Constantinopolitan archiepiscopate. But the rivalry and the opposition were motivated more by personal ambition than by theological difference. As an exegete he belongs essentially to the same Antiochene tradition as his greater rival.

Many of these fourth-century commentators were very closely involved in the Arian and Christological controversies of their day. Their work of commentary was not detached from their work of doctrinal definition; their particular Christological concerns did much to mould the detail of their exegesis. Nevertheless, there is much in the Pauline epistles which is only indirectly related to the subjects of the great fourth-century controversies. On such issues as law and grace or faith and works, doctrinal opponents were often exegetically at one. So it was also with the great rival schools of Alexandria and Antioch. Some of the differences in interpretation do correspond to the traditional division between those two great schools of exegesis. But this is by no means always the case. The basic divergence between an allegorical and a more literal approach to Scripture is far less relevant to the interpretation of Paul's writings than it is to that of the Old Testament or of the Gospels. So although the varieties of exegesis are many and interesting, we may come nearer with the Pauline epistles than with any other major portion of the Scriptures to speaking legitimately of a Greek tradition of exegesis.

But the Greeks were not the only early commentators. If they were first in the field, none the less we have five sets of Latin commentaries from between the years A.D. 360 and A.D. 410, all of which are of considerable interest and worth. We must turn our attention now therefore to the situation of those Western writers.

We know nothing of any Latin commentaries from the ante-Nicene period, from the years when Clement and Origen were starting the Greeks upon the road of Pauline commentary in Alexandria. Nevertheless, that early period was of almost as much importance for the history of Pauline exegesis in the Western as in the Eastern half of the Christian world. The work of Irenaeus and of Tertullian, though not taking the form of the writing of commentaries, was most intimately bound up with many of the fundamental problems arising in the interpretation of Paul's writings. More firmly and more uncompromisingly than their Eastern counterparts, they ensured that the words of Paul would be read and understood in a manner radically opposed to Gnostic or Marcionite ways of thought. When in due course the writing of commentaries in the West began, that issue was already firmly settled and no doubts upon it ever troubled the minds of the commentators.

The five men from whose pens we have Latin commentaries were all people of unusual attainments and interests. The earliest was Marius Victorinus, and we possess his commentaries on Galatians, Philippians and Ephesians, probably composed soon after the year A.D. 360. Victorinus was a convert to Christianity in adult life, having been a distinguished professor of rhetoric and a Neoplatonist philosopher. As a Christian he was an ardent champion of the anti-Arian cause, and this seems to have been a major motive for the writing of his commentaries. Thus he combined orthodoxy of doctrinal belief with an intellectual background which stood right outside the Church and the main stream of Christian tradition. This is clearly evident in his commentaries, which show an interesting and unusual independence of treatment when compared with the majority of the other patristic commentaries.

The second of our five commentators is perhaps the most important of them all, and yet his name is not known to us. The name by which he is called is Ambrosiaster, because for many centuries his works were preserved under the name of Ambrose and until the time of Erasmus were regarded as genuine works of the bishop of Milan. They were written during the pontificate of Damasus (A.D. 366–84), and for the first time we have to do with a complete set of commentaries on all the Pauline epistles apparently conceived and executed as a unity. Many attempts have been made to identify the author, but no suggestion is free from difficulty. That which has found most favour is Isaac, the converted Jew, who was a lawyer and vigorous opponent of Damasus. It is tempting to identify the author of the first full-scale commentary on Paul's letters with one who was himself a convert from Judaism, but the identification cannot be regarded as more than a possible conjecture. Whoever he was, his work is remarkably succinct and complete for one who was still essentially a pioneer in the field of Latin commentary.

Whatever be the true solution to the mystery of the person of Ambrosiaster, the three remaining commentators are all men whose names are written large upon the pages of contemporary history. Jerome was undoubtedly the greatest biblical scholar of his age. We possess his commentaries on Galatians, Ephesians and Philemon. These were written between the years A.D. 387 and A.D. 389, soon after Jerome had settled at Bethlehem and before the outbreak of the first great Origenist controversy. Thus geographical and historical circumstance combined with his great linguistic knowledge to make him ideally situated to enter into the heritage of the Greek commentators.

And that is precisely what he did. Victorinus is the only Latin predecessor whom he acknowledges, and him he dismisses as eloquent but ignorant of the Scriptures.[1] Of Ambrosiaster's work he shows no knowledge. If Ambrosiaster was in fact Isaac, the opponent of Jerome's patron Damasus, then Jerome's ignoring of his work would not be difficult to understand; it could well be deliberate. But upon earlier Greek writers he drew extensively. He acknowledges his debt particularly to Origen,[2] and there can be no question but that his commentaries are very closely based upon those of Origen.[3] Jerome's work is certainly thorough and erudite, but it has the air of a compilation of Greek learning rather than of a genuinely original Latin composition.

If Jerome was the greatest biblical scholar of his age, Augustine was its greatest theologian. The only three works of direct Pauline commentary from Augustine's pen belong to a comparatively early stage of his literary career. The three works are of differing natures. They consist of a commentary on Galatians, an exposition of certain selected statements from Romans, and the start of what would have been a massive commentary on Romans but which never proceeded beyond a treatment of the salutation, the opening seven verses of the first chapter. All these were written during the time of his presbyterate, around the year A.D. 394, a time when the central emphasis in Augustine's writing was just beginning to move from philosophical to more biblical ways of thought. Although in his later writings Augustine did not resume the directly exegetical treatment of the Pauline epistles, there is much in those later works also which is of outstanding importance in the history of Pauline exegesis.

Finally we have to set beside the work of Augustine a complete set of commentaries from the pen of his great theological opponent, Pelagius. These were written in about A.D. 406–9 and come therefore, like Augustine's works of direct Pauline commentary, from a time before the outbreak of the Pelagian controversy. They consist for the most part of extremely brief explanatory notes on the text of the epistles. Yet for all the brevity of his comments Pelagius

---

[1] Jerome, *Comm. in Gal.* Prolog. (308 A).   [2] *Ibid.* (308 B).

[3] See A. Harnack, *Der kirchengeschichtliche Ertrag der exegetischen Arbeiten des Origenes* (1919), pt 2, pp. 141–68.

reveals a wide knowledge of the earlier commentaries and draws extensively not only upon his Latin predecessors but also upon the tradition of Greek exegesis. He knew Origen's commentary on Romans in Rufinus' translation and shows close affinities with the later Antiochene exegetes, especially Theodore of Mopsuestia. The relation between them is not easy to determine, but it seems most likely that Pelagius is the borrower. In many ways his work supplies a summary conspectus of the exegetical struggles of the preceding years.

So in the three and a half centuries after Paul first wrote his letters of missionary correction and of exhortation to the newly founded churches of his day, there grew up an extensive literature in interpretation of those letters, engaging the activity of some of the ablest minds of the period. Moreover, the prosecution of that work of interpretation was no mere matter of antiquarian concern. It was an integral part of a total continuing attempt to understand the full significance of God's revelation in Christ. To this day differences in the interpretation of Paul's teaching are an important factor in the continuing division between Catholic and Protestant understandings of the faith. Thus the study of the earliest exegesis of Paul's writings cannot but have important bearings both upon the history of doctrine and upon the ecumenical problems of our own day.[1]

---

[1] Cf. J. N. Sanders's review of K. H. Schelkle, *Paulus Lehrer der Väter*, in *J.T.S.* n.s. VIII (1957), 316.

CHAPTER II

THE APOSTLE

The exaltation of the Pauline letters to the rank of Christian Scriptures necessarily involved a high view of the person of their author and of the divine inspiration determining and guiding their composition. It is, as we should expect, with Origen, the first systematic commentator upon the letters, that such ideas begin to be developed in a thoroughgoing way. According to Origen, it is Christ, living in the apostles, who speaks in the apostolic letters. Not one jot or tittle within them therefore is superfluous; every detail must be treated as of importance.[1] This belief is one that was shared by all the subsequent commentators of the early Church. Thus Didymus interprets Paul's words in II Cor. i. 13, that 'we write nothing other than you can read and know', as implying the claim that his words are consistent with those of Moses, the prophets and the evangelists and that they are inspired in the same sense.[2] Chrysostom can cite a word of Christ from the gospel and follow it with a word of Paul, which he claims is equally a word of Christ because it is Christ who directs Paul's mind.[3] Both he and Jerome know of those who claim that it was not in everything Paul wrote or said that Christ was speaking and that the Epistle to Philemon is too trivial to warrant its place in the canon. But neither has the slightest hesitation in dismissing such claims absolutely. Every word of the apostle, every detail about his life, is of great value to the Christian.[4]

Thus the fundamental assertion that the real spokesman of the epistles is Christ as truly as it is Paul was common to all the commentators throughout our period. At first, however, it was not held

---

[1] Origen, *Frag. in Matt.* 218 (*G.C.S.* ed. Klostermann, p. 104); *Comm. in Rom.* 2, 6 (883 B) on Rom. ii. 8; *ibid.* 9, 41 (1243 B) on Rom. xiv. 11–13; *ibid.* 10, 25 (1281 B) on Rom. xvi. 10.

[2] Didymus on II Cor. i. 13 (Staab, p. 17). Cf. also Didymus on II Cor. xii. 4 (Staab, p. 41).

[3] Chr. *Comm. in Gal.* 1, 7 (10, 624) on Gal. i. 9.

[4] Chr. *Hom. in Philemon*, Arg. (11, 702–4); Jerome, *Comm. in Philemon*, Prolog. (599 D–602 D).

with quite the same degree of absoluteness as in the later years of the fourth century. Thus Origen, for example, does find in Paul's letters an element of purely personal judgement on Paul's part, which while it by no means altogether undermines their authority does put it at a distinguishably lower level than the more directly divine authority of the prophets or the gospels.[1] He is particularly impressed by the careful differentiation which Paul himself draws in his teaching on marriage in I Cor. vii between what is his own injunction and what is the word of the Lord. This leads him to the belief that, just as in the laws of Moses we are to distinguish between those which are the eternal laws of God and those which are only the laws of Moses himself and which are sometimes even contrary to the former, so in the New Testament we are to distinguish between the gospels and the secondary inferior laws of the apostle.[2] Tertullian, at least in his Montanist phase, goes even further. It is true that in the *De Corona* he speaks of Paul as giving counsel, where he had no explicit command of the Lord, under the guidance of the Spirit who leads into all truth, and describes that counsel as equivalent to a divine command.[3] But in some of his other Montanist writings he draws the distinction even more strongly than Origen. Paul's concession is based on no commandment of God; it is a merely human counsel, deriving from his own merely human way of looking at things. None the less he does not, as he clearly could not, simply denounce Paul's words; they were required by the exigencies of the time, but are open to be revoked by the Paraclete. Thus even in his ultra-Montanist phase Tertullian clearly regards every word of Paul as fully binding on the Christian unless explicitly revoked by some later revelation of divine authority.[4] Chrysostom, however, writes at a time when the veneration for Paul has had two more centuries in which to grow, and he is unwilling to compromise in any way his firm belief that Christ is the true author of the epistles in their totality. When Paul draws his distinction in I Cor. vii between those injunctions which are not his but the Lord's and

[1] Origen, *Comm. in Joann.* i, 3.
[2] Origen, Frag. on I Cor. vii. 10 (*J.T.S.* ix, 505).
[3] *De Corona*, 4, 6.
[4] *De Exhortatione Castitatis*, 4; *De Monogamia*, 3 and 14 (I Cor. vii. 25, 9–10).

those which are his and not the Lord's, he does not really mean to imply that the latter group are any less truly commands of Christ than the former. The distinction relates solely to the method of their transmission. The former group are the words of Christ incarnate, the latter the words of Christ speaking in and through Paul; there is no difference of divine authority between the two.[1] Similarly, Paul's claim in I Thess. iv. 14 that what he is declaring to them is 'by the word of the Lord' is motivated not so much by any special authority for this particular declaration as by the strangeness of the nature of the declaration, which therefore required a special reminder of his permanent authority in order to ensure its reception. The prophets had declared 'the word of the Lord' as it came to them in external vision; Paul had Christ speaking in him.[2]

This assertion that the words of Paul in his letters are really the words of Christ was certainly felt to be consistent with a recognition of the difficulty and even the imperfection of their form. Thus when Origen, like the author of II Peter, refers to the variety of conflicting interpretations of Paul's meaning, he gives as one reason the weakness of Paul's powers of self-expression.[3] Three lines of argument are used in explanation of this fact. The first consists of an appeal to Paul's own avowed description of himself in II Cor. xi. 6 as 'rude in speech' (ἰδιώτης τῷ λόγῳ). The words are frequently quoted by Origen to account for apparent grammatical or syntactical inaccuracies.[4] Jerome uses this line of reasoning to explain the obscurity of Col. ii. 18–19,[5] and Chrysostom regards it as a fundamental characteristic of Paul's writing.[6] Chrysostom indeed goes much further and even speaks of Paul as only able to speak Hebrew[7] and incapable of writing Greek letters clearly.[8] Jerome ridicules

---

[1] Chr. *De Virginitate*, 12 (I Cor. vii. 10, 12).

[2] Chr. *Hom. in I Thess.* 7, 1 (11, 436) and 8, 1 (11, 439) on I Thess. iv. 14 (II Cor. xiii. 3). Cf. Theod. on I Thess. iv. 14 (Swete, 11, 28).

[3] Origen on Rom. iv. 23 (Scherer, p. 218).

[4] Origen, *ibid.*; Frags. on Eph. ii. 1, iii. 1 and iii. 13 (*J.T.S.* iii, 403, 408, 409). Cf. Jerome on Gal. iii. 1 (347B); on Gal. vi. 1 (426C).

[5] Jerome, *Ep.* 121, 10.

[6] Chr. *Hom. in Rom.* Praef. (9, 394); *De Sacerdotio*, 4.

[7] Chr. *Hom. in II Tim.* 4, 3 (11, 622).

[8] Chr. *Comm. in Gal.* 6, 3 (10, 678) on Gal. vi. 11.

this last suggestion;[1] he speaks highly of Paul's knowledge of Hebrew and of the law but does admit the imperfection of his Greek[2] and regards him as having only a moderate knowledge of secular literature.[3] Theodore of Mopsuestia also comments on the lack of grammatical or rhetorical skill in the composition of the epistles.[4] Yet all such apparent disparagement of Paul's literary abilities served only to enhance the grace of God, which could use so unskilled a writer to so great effect.[5] Origen is the most frequent, even though not the most extreme, exponent of such ideas (most of the references in Jerome can safely be traced back to him), yet he is not altogether happy with them. He finds in the letters subtle varieties of wording and forceful use of argument in spite of Paul's disclaimer.[6] Paul, in fact, uses the principles of dialectic naturally; the learned art of dialectic is after all only the codification of man's natural and customary ways of thinking.[7] Furthermore, he suggests, Paul deliberately plays down his own learning in order to ensure that it is his message rather than his own wisdom which will command men's attention.[8] A second line of argument is to claim that some of the obscurities in Paul's writings are to be attributed to the rapidity of his discourse under the powerful impetus of the Spirit and to his desire to express so great doctrines in so small a compass.[9] But thirdly some apparent obscurities, inconsistencies or imperfections in the argument are deliberate. Thus for Origen the difficulties occasioned by the rapidly changing meaning of the word 'law' in Rom. vii are the result of Paul's deliberate desire to conceal the truths of God from the merely flippant, who are not prepared to devote serious study to them.[10] Jerome interprets the words

---

[1] Jerome on Gal. vi. 11 (434).

[2] Jerome on Gal. iii. 10 (357C); on Gal. vi. 1 (426C); *Ep.* 120, 11.

[3] Jerome on Gal. iv. 24 (389C).   [4] Theod. on I Tim. i. 3 (Swete, II, 70).

[5] Jerome on Eph. iii. 1 (478). For similar comments on the writings of St John by Origen, see M. F. Wiles, *The Spiritual Gospel* (1960), p. 10.

[6] Origen, *Comm. in Rom.* 4, 11 (999B, C) on Rom. v. 8–9.

[7] Origen, Frag. on I Cor. xv. 14 (*J.T.S.* x, 45).

[8] Origen, *Comm. in Rom.* 6, 13 (1098A) on Rom. viii. 9–11.

[9] Irenaeus, *Adv. Haer.* 3, 7, 2 (Harvey, II, 26); Chr. *Hom. in Eph.* 11, 3 (11, 84) on Eph. iv. 14–16; Theod. on Eph. iii. 1 (Swete, I, 155).

[10] Origen, *Comm. in Rom.* 6, 8 (1076C–1079A) on Rom. vii. 7–13. This is of course in keeping with Origen's general beliefs about the outer form of Scripture as a whole (cf. *Con. Cel.* 6, 18).

κατὰ ἄνθρωπον in Gal. iii. 15 as implying 'fitting the Galatians' low level of intellect' and admits that the argument which follows is not strictly valid from a scholarly point of view.[1] Chrysostom develops this point in a more positive manner. Paul's aim is not to produce a perfectly ordered discourse, but to win over and build up the very mixed and very imperfect members of the churches to whom he is writing. Thus if the simile of the married woman in Rom. vii. 1–3 seems to be imperfectly applied, this is due to Paul's desire not to press the point too heavily upon his readers.[2] If Paul's argument in II Corinthians seems at times to lack logical sequence and even consistency, it is all to be explained in terms of the varieties of good and bad within the Church and the tactfulness of Paul's approach to them.[3] In fact Paul's own words in that very letter that 'if we are beside ourselves it is for God; if we are in our right mind it is for you' are to be understood as a direct affirmation of this principle in his letter-writing activity.[4]

Paul himself is, as we should expect, described in terms of the highest praise. With Irenaeus and Tertullian, however, this praise is tempered with caution. Even though Tertullian's description of him as 'haereticorum apostolus' was not intended to imply any kind of disparagement,[5] yet they could never forget the use to which his writings had been put by Marcion. It would be altogether wrong to reject Paul's apostleship completely as the Ebionites did,[6] but it was equally disastrous to contrast him with the other apostles as the only one with a clear knowledge of the truth. Paul himself bears clear testimony to his fundamental unity with them.[7] His claim to a more abundant labour than theirs refers only to the more difficult nature of the missionary task to the Gentiles.[8] In fact he

---

[1] Jerome on Gal. iii. 15 (364B–365A). Jerome probably derives this point directly from Origen.

[2] Chr. *Hom. in Rom.* 12, 2 (9, 497) on Rom. vii. 2–3.

[3] Chr. *Hom. in II Cor.* 14, 2 (10, 499) on II Cor. vii. 2–4; *ibid.* 16, 2 (10, 513) on II Cor. viii. 1; *ibid.* 21, 1 (10, 541) on II Cor. x. 1. Chrysostom uses a very similar argument in his interpretation of the words of Jesus in the gospels (cf. M. F. Wiles, *The Spiritual Gospel*, pp. 139–40).

[4] Chr. *De Laudibus Pauli Apostoli*, 5 (II Cor. v. 13).

[5] Tertullian, *Adv. Marc.* 3, 5, 4. [6] Irenaeus, *Adv. Haer.* 3, 15, 1 (Harvey, II, 79).

[7] *Ibid.* 3, 13, 1 (Harvey, II, 72–3) (Gal. ii. 8; I Cor. xv. 11).

[8] *Ibid.* 4, 24, 1 (Harvey, II, 231). Cf. Ambst. on Gal. ii. 8 (349B).

did give way to them in subjection;[1] his difference with Peter described in the second half of Gal. ii was on a comparatively minor issue.[2] Paul's behaviour was that of an overzealous neophyte, still in the rudiments of grace, and later on he himself came to adopt a more tolerant attitude to Judaism, as his declaration that he was prepared to become a Jew to the Jews bears witness.[3] It may well be that Peter's action at Antioch was based on this selfsame principle of accommodation, which Paul later came to adopt.[4]

Clement and Origen feel no such inhibitions about their commendation of Paul; still less do the writers of later generations. Clement is aware that there are those who are uncertain about the true status of the 'divine apostle', as he himself calls him, but for his own part he has no doubt that his teaching is soundly rooted in the Old Testament.[5] The problem of his conflict with Peter is dealt with by the drastic expedient of asserting that the Cephas in question was one of the seventy and not the chief apostle at all.[6] For Origen, Paul follows Jesus as the founder of the churches in Christ;[7] he is the greatest of the apostles,[8] especially in point of wisdom.[9] He never subjected himself to the other apostles;[10] in his argument with Peter both were right and the element of quarrel is glossed over.[11] He was endowed with the special prophetic gift of knowledge of what is happening at a distance like Elisha.[12] If he appears at times in his epistles to speak of his own moral weaknesses and failures, these are not to be understood as referring directly to

[1] Irenaeus, *Adv. Haer.* 3, 13, 3 (Harvey, II, 74). Tertullian appears to accuse Marcion of adding the negative to the text of Gal. ii. 5 in order to achieve the opposite sense (*Adv. Marc.* 5, 3, 3).

[2] Tertullian, *op. cit.* 5, 3, 7 (Gal. ii. 11–21).

[3] *Ibid.* 1, 20, 2–3 (Gal. ii. 2, 11–21; I Cor. ix. 20–2).

[4] *Ibid.* 4, 3, 3; *De Praescriptione*, 24, 2.

[5] Clement, *Stromateis*, 6, 21, 13 (cf. C. Bigg, *Christian Platonists of Alexandria* (1913), p. 81).

[6] Clement in Eusebius, *H.E.* 1, 12, 2.   [7] Origen, *Con. Cel.* 1, 63.

[8] Origen, *Hom. in Num.* 3, 3.

[9] Origen, *Sel. in Ps.* ii. 1 (*P.G.* 12, 1101 B).

[10] Origen, *Con. Cel.* 7, 21 (Gal. ii. 5).

[11] *Ibid.* 2, 1. Cf. *Comm. in Joann.* 32, 5. For a fuller discussion of Origen's view on this vexed question see p. 22 n. 1 below.

[12] Origen, Frag. on I Cor. v. 3 (*J.T.S.* IX, 364). Cf. Ambst. on Col. ii. 5 (428 A), Pelagius on I Cor. v. 3 (p. 151), and Chr. *Hom. in I Cor.* 15, 2 (10, 123), on I Cor. v. 3.

himself; rather he applies to himself (as David and Daniel had done in the Old Testament) what is really true only of the weak convert.[1] He does not need, like the Ephesian Christians, to have his feet shod for the journey to the Holy Land; he is one of those apostles for whom Christ declared no shoes to be needed because they were already perfected and living in the Holy Land.[2] The description of present tribulation as light and momentary is true not of everyone but only of Paul and those like him who have the perfect love of God shed abroad in their hearts by the Holy Spirit.[3] His claim to be 'free from all' implies a freedom from every kind of sin, which is true only of a 'perfect' (τέλειος) apostle.[4]

On another occasion, however, Origen does allow for a spiritual development, whereby Paul grows to higher levels of perfection. In Phil. iii. 12–13 Paul openly admits that he has not yet attained perfection.[5] His progress, Origen asserts, can be traced in the differing spiritual conditions revealed by autobiographical remarks in the different epistles. In I Corinthians he still fears he may be rejected; in Philippians he is still genuinely doubtful whether he will attain the resurrection from the dead; in II Corinthians he has reached the higher stage of always bearing about in his body the dying of Jesus, while in Romans he is more than conqueror in all things and nothing can separate him from the love of God.[6] But more often Origen speaks in simple and unqualified terms of

[1] Origen, *Comm. in Rom.* 6, 9 (1089 C–1090 C) on Rom. vii. 14–25.

[2] Origen, Frag. on Eph. vi. 15 (*J.T.S.* III, 574). The Old Testament basis for this allegorical distinction is to be found in the contrasting injunctions of Exod. xii. 11 on the one hand and Exod. iii. 5 and Josh. v. 15 on the other.

[3] Origen, *Comm. in Can. Cantic.* Prolog. (*G.C.S.* ed. Baehrens, p. 73). The references are to II Cor. iv. 17 and Rom. v. 5, with the significant addition of the word 'perfect' to the latter text.

[4] Origen, Frag. on I Cor. ix. 19 (*J.T.S.* IX, 512). See also Origen, *Comm. in Joann.* 20, 26, according to which the 'we who are alive' of I Thess. iv. 15 is a spiritual classification representing οἱ τετελειωμένοι καὶ μηδαμῶς ἔτι ἁμαρτίαν ἐργαζόμενοι, and Paul is fully conscious of belonging to this class.

[5] Origen argues that the immediately ensuing affirmation of perfection in *v.* 15 is evidence that the word is being used in two different senses. Pelagius (p. 408) uses it to prove that Paul's denial of perfection in his own case is a matter of humility and not of fact.

[6] Origen, *Comm. in Rom.* Praef. (833 B–835 B) (I Cor. ix. 27; Phil. iii. 11; II Cor. iv. 8–10; Rom. viii. 35–9).

Paul's perfection, and it is worthy of note that he can base this belief on words from the very same chapter of I Corinthians as that which he also used to illustrate the lowest stage of Paul's spiritual progress. The idea of a gradual spiritual development is never really integrated into the main body of his thought about Paul's person.[1]

Certainly the kind of adulation which involves the assertion of an unqualified moral perfection continued to increase both in frequency and in intensity with the passage of the years. Before we turn to the full flower of this conception in the writings of Chrysostom, an interesting example of the developing idea may be cited from the *De Resurrectione* of Methodius, who was bishop of Olympus at the beginning of the fourth century. Methodius is concerned with the famous 'Pauline confession' of Rom. vii. Unlike Origen, he assumes that Paul is here speaking of his own experience. But if so, he argues, it must be interpreted in a way which does not involve the attribution of any sin to Paul, for Paul could never have said that we should be imitators of him as he was of Christ unless his life was an exact imitation of Christ free from all sin. Methodius is therefore forced to interpret the words 'the good that I would I do not, the evil that I would not that I do' as referring not to actions but only to the realm of thought, which does not come within the range of man's free-will and therefore carries no culpability with it.[2]

[1] A similar inconsistency, which doubtless goes back to Origen, is apparent in Jerome's Commentary on Galatians. In commenting on Gal. iv. 29 (395 B, C) he uses Origen's interpretation of I Cor. ix. 19 to prove that Paul was free from all sin. A little later on (405 D) he expresses doubt as to the compatibility of Paul's sentiments in Gal. v. 12 with the spirit of Christ and suggests that Paul, being after all only human, may at this point have been led into sin by that other law at work in his members. This doubtless derives from Origen also, although it is tempting to detect a trace of self-knowledge on the part of Jerome when he says that to curse one's enemies is a sin 'in quod frequenter sanctos viros cadere perspicimus'. In typically Origenistic fashion Jerome allows the possibility of an alternative exegesis of the verse, according to which it is a prayer in the spirit of Matt. xviii. 8–9. Augustine gives a similar interpretation but links it with Matt. xix. 12 (*Expos. Gal.* 42 on Gal. v. 4–12).

[2] Methodius, *De Resurrectione*, 2, 4, 1–5 (Rom. vii. 19; I Cor. xi. 1). Didymus more simply uses I Cor. xi. 1 as evidence that Rom. vii does not refer to Paul at all (Staab, p. 1). Augustine originally took the passage as about the experience of man

So the way is prepared for the full and passionate expression which later writers, and especially Chrysostom, give to these praises of Paul. The basic difficulty of the quarrel with Peter is overcome by the supposition that the whole affair was deliberately staged in order to win over the Jerusalem party.[1] Paul did not go up to Jerusalem to satisfy any doubts of his own about the rightness of his conduct; it was his opponents whom he wished to convince that he had not run in vain.[2] His claim to be crucified to the world is a claim to be entirely free from all human 'passion' (πάθος).[3] His thorn in the flesh or messenger of Satan could not have been an illness of the head imposed by Satan, for Satan could not have had such authority over the body of one who could determine Satan's control over the bodies of others, as in the case of the incestuous person at Corinth. It must have been something more external to Paul himself, and should be understood of the activities of his

before grace, but later changed his mind (*Expos. Prop. Ep. ad Rom.* 44 on Rom. vii. 19–20; *Retractationes*, I, 23, 1). In so far as he links it explicitly with Paul's experience as a Christian he follows a line similar to that of Methodius by interpreting the failure to do what he wills as the experience of a feeling of lust and not as any action resulting from it (*Sermo*, 151, 6).

[1] Chr. *Comm. in Gal.* 2, 4 (10, 640) on Gal. ii. 11–12; *In illud, in faciem Petro restiti* (*P.G.* 51, 371 ff.). This was also the view of Jerome, who attributes its inception to Origen in the tenth book of the *Stromateis* (*Ep.* 112, 6). It does not however appear to have been Origen's mature and considered view, since he makes no use of it in *Con. Cel.* 2, 1, where it would have served him well if he still held to it. Indeed it is possible that he had already abandoned it by the time he wrote his commentary on Galatians, which cannot be dated with any certainty but which probably belongs, unlike the *Stromateis*, to his Caesarean period. Jerome in the introduction to his commentary (308 B) claims to be using both Origen's commentary and the tenth book of the *Stromateis*. He puts forward the 'staged' interpretation in comment on Gal. ii. 11 (339–40) and when challenged refers only to the tenth book of Origen's *Stromateis* as his basic source. Moreover, his earlier comments on Gal. ii. 6 (335) seem to imply a real quarrel. Perhaps in that instance he is relying on Origen's commentary, and the 'staged' interpretation did not appear there. Jerome also himself seems to have abandoned the idea in later life (*Adv. Pel.* 1, 22). In his case the stinging criticism of Augustine must have played a major part in any change of mind (see pp. 25 and 71–2 below). For a full discussion of the patristic interpretation of this question see J. B. Lightfoot, *Epistle of St Paul to the Galatians* (1890), pp. 128–32.

[2] Chr. *Comm. in Gal.* 2, 1 (10, 633–4) on Gal. ii. 2; Jerome on Gal. ii. 2 (333 C); Theod. on Gal. ii. 2 (Swete, 1, 16). Augustine goes further and says that it was not even for the sake of those with whom he was conferring but for those to whom he was writing (*Expos. Gal.* 10 on Gal. ii. 1–2).

[3] Chr. *De Laudibus Pauli Apostoli*, 2 (Gal. vi. 14).

opponents.[1] He enjoyed a measure of communion with God such as was given to no other prophet or apostle. That he speaks little of it is due to his humility; when he speaks of it at all, he does so only because the attacks of false apostles make it imperative, and even then he uses a deliberately indirect manner of speaking.[2] Any apparent admission of moral failing is to be explained by the principle which Origen had used of applying to himself what is strictly applicable only to less mature Christians. Paul did not need the thorn in the flesh to learn humility or the experience of the sentence of death in Asia in order to learn to trust God rather than himself. It is entirely for the sake of others that he draws out these lessons from his experience and speaks as if he himself had needed to learn them.[3]

Chrysostom clearly contemplates the application of this principle to other admissions of non-moral limitations on Paul's part, but does not find it necessary to do so. Paul really did not know what to pray for as he ought, as his praying about his thorn in the flesh bears out.[4] His ignorance reminds us that he was truly a man and makes him thereby a more valuable example for us.[5] He really was afraid, but that only enhances the nobility of his achievements.[6]

When God created the stars and the sun, the angels of God sang for joy; but it was with yet greater joy that they hailed God's gift of Paul to the world.[7] Such is the idyllic praise of which Chrysostom finds him worthy. In particular it is the humility of Paul which attracts him and to which he continually draws our attention.[8] Theodore indeed suggests that part of the value of the inclusion of

---

[1] Chr. *Hom. in II Cor.* 26, 2 (10, 577–8) on II Cor. xii. 7 (I Cor. v. 5). For a recent tendency to return to this type of interpretation, see J. Y. Mullins, 'Paul's Thorn in the Flesh', *J.B.L.* LXXVI, pt iv (Dec. 1957), 299–303, and J. Munck, *Paulus und die Heilsgeschichte* (1954), p. 319 n. 13 (E.T. p. 325 n. 2).

[2] Chr. *De Laudibus Pauli Apostoli*, 5 (II Cor. xii. 2, 5, 11).

[3] Chr. *Hom. in II Cor.* 2, 2–3 (10, 395) on II Cor. i. 9 (II Cor. xii. 7).

[4] Chr. *Hom. in Rom.* 14, 7 (9, 532–3) on Rom. viii. 26.

[5] Chr. *Hom. in I Thess.* 4, 1 (11, 415–16) on I Thess. iii. 5.

[6] Chr. *Hom. in I Cor.* 6, 1 (10, 49) on I Cor. ii. 3; *De Laudibus Pauli Apostoli*, 6.

[7] Chr. *Hom. in Phil.* 4, 1 (11, 206) on Phil. i. 22–6.

[8] E.g. Chr. *Hom. in I Cor.* 38, 5 (10, 328–9) on I Cor. xv. 10; *Hom. in II Cor.* 1, 3 (10, 386) on II Cor. i. 3–4; *ibid.* 8, 3 (10, 456) on II Cor. iv. 5; *Comm. in Gal.* 1, 11 (10, 631) on Gal. i. 17; *Hom. in Col.* 11, 3 (11, 377) on Col. iv. 9; *Hom. in I Thess.* 11, 2 (11, 463) on I Thess. v. 25.

the Epistle to Philemon within the canon lies in its vivid portrayal of Paul's humility not merely in relation to a church but even in a purely personal matter.[1] As a comparison of I Cor. xi. 1 and Eph. v. 1–2 makes clear, it was love which stood at the heart of Paul's *imitatio Christi*.[2] And, as Origen with his customary insight had pointed out long before, at no point does Paul express that *imitatio Christi* in the way of love more completely than in declaring himself ready to be accursed for his brethren's sake, just as his master had been made a curse for us.[3]

Paul in fact represents for Chrysostom the supreme example of the moral and spiritual potentialities of human life. He lived in the same world as we do, shared our nature and had a body subject to all the same limitations as ours. What the grace of God achieved in the life of Paul, it can achieve in us. No greater incentive to holy living could be desired or conceived.[4] There is, it may well be claimed, a remarkable similarity between Chrysostom's picture of Paul and the Jesus of liberal scholarship and piety. No moral failing must be admitted in the drawing of the picture; a limitation of knowledge is admitted with some reluctance; other human limitations are more gladly accepted as emphasizing both a oneness with ordinary men and the wonder of the life that shines through them. Perhaps the exalted Christology of the period even at Antioch tended to destroy the sense of Christ's solidarity with us and the force of his life as a human example, thus leaving a gap in popular piety which this stress on the achievements of Paul may have helped to fill.[5]

This extreme development was a characteristic of Eastern Christianity. The West was far more guarded and restrained in its evaluation of the apostles. Victorinus in particular is remarkable for the candid nature of his comments on the early apostles. Not only

---

[1] Theod. *Comm. in Philemon*, Arg. (Swete, II, 266).

[2] Chr. *De Laudibus Pauli Apostoli*, 3.

[3] Origen, *Comm. in Rom.* 7, 13 (1138 C) on Rom. ix. 2; Frag. on I Cor. xiii. 5 (*J.T.S.* x, 35); Jerome on Gal. v. 14 (410 A). For detailed references to later writers who follow Origen on this point see K. H. Schelkle, *Paulus Lehrer der Väter*, p. 328.

[4] Chr. *De Laudibus Pauli Apostoli*, 2, 4 and 5.

[5] Cf. the remarks of H. Chadwick in 'Eucharist and Christology in the Nestorian controversy', *J.T.S.* n.s. II (1951), 163–4, about the causes of the rise in the position attributed to Mary about this period.

was Peter in the wrong living temporarily as a Jew out of fear, but James was preaching a wrongly Jewish Christianity of heretical character.[1] Even Paul, in spite of all he did and suffered for Christ, is not to be thought of as perfected while still in this life, as his words in Phil. iii. 13 bear out.[2] The difference of approach between East and West stands out most clearly in the different premises from which they argue in discussing the story of Paul's rebuke of Peter. The controversy between Jerome and Augustine on the subject was in effect a controversy between East and West. Jerome explicitly claims to be writing in continuation of the tradition of the Greek commentators,[3] while Augustine quotes in his defence the authority of Cyprian and Ambrose.[4] Jerome is not concerned to defend his theory of a deliberately staged quarrel to the last ditch, but he is concerned to insist that it is incumbent upon his opponents to provide some alternative explanation in which no blame can be attached either to Peter or to Paul.[5] Theodore was clearly guided by the same basic assumption when, in allowing the possibility of either the staged or the natural interpretation of the quarrel, he insists that in either case both apostles come well out of it.[6] But Augustine did not feel the same necessity to maintain the perfection of the apostles' conduct. It is more reasonable in his view to suppose that Peter the apostle erred, as men of God like David had done, than to allow that the record of Scripture is either deceptive or untrue. It is the words of the apostles recorded in Scripture rather than their lives which must be treated as wholly reliable.[7] In the West more easily than in the East the admiration and honour directed towards the persons of the apostles could be allowed to fall short of the assertion of their perfection.

[1] Victorinus on Gal. ii. 12 (1162B–1163C); on Gal. i. 13–14 (1153C); on Gal. i. 19 (1155B–1156B).
[2] Victorinus on Phil. iii. 13 (1221).
[3] Jerome, *Ep.* 112, 4.
[4] *Ibid.* 116, 24.
[5] Jerome on Gal. ii. 14 (342A); *Ep.* 112, 4.
[6] Theod. on Gal. ii. 11–14 (Swete, I, 22–3).
[7] Jerome, *Ep.* 116, 5–7.

CHAPTER III

THE NATURE OF MAN

'In my flesh dwelleth no good thing.' 'They that are in the flesh cannot please God.' 'The flesh lusteth against the Spirit.'[1] In the light of such texts as these it is hardly surprising that interpreters of Paul are continually tempted to ascribe to him a fundamentally dualistic understanding of man's nature, according to which his physical nature as such is evil. That certainly was how the Gnostics interpreted him. Gnostic exegesis of Scripture in general tends to be fanciful and almost wholly arbitrary in character. In some measure that is true of their exegesis on this particular theme. The Encratite Cassianus, for example, interpreted the sowing to the flesh which reaps corruption of Gal. vi. 8 quite literally as the transmission of seed in sexual intercourse, and so used the saying as an argument to prove the sinfulness of any form of sexual intercourse.[2] But Gnostic exegesis did not need to be wholly tendentious in order to claim the support of the great apostle for their belief in the evil character of man's bodily nature. There is sufficient ambiguity, at least at the surface level of Paul's writing, to make it a plausible interpretation of his mind, and the Gnostics have never been without their successors in later generations who have come to the same conclusion as they did. Certainly the would-be interpreter of Paul has to face the issue of what Paul's attitude to the body really was and make a conscious decision about it. The Gnostic use of Paul's letters forced the Church to do that quickly and decisively.

Irenaeus and Tertullian are the earliest orthodox writers whose work survives in substantial quantity. They were particularly concerned with the issues of Gnosticism and they insist that the Gnostic interpretation is not a true understanding of Paul's teaching. Tertullian recognizes the force of the Gnostic argument but counters

[1] Rom. vii. 18; viii. 8; Gal. v. 17.
[2] Jerome on Gal. vi. 8 (431 A, B). Jerome (or Origen, on whom he is almost certainly dependent at this point) replies by pointing out that Paul speaks of sowing to one's *own* flesh.

it on two scores. In the first place it takes no account of a second element in Paul's letters, which shows the potentialities of flesh as a vehicle for the glory of God. Our bodies are 'members of Christ', they are the 'temple of God' and we are to glorify God in them.[1] Secondly, the apparently disparaging remarks about the flesh in Paul's writing are to be understood not of its substance but of its actions.[2] This basic insight, having been once firmly established, becomes an underlying principle of interpretation for all subsequent commentators. Thus we find the same contrast between substance and actions recurring, for example, in Chrysostom's exegesis of Rom. vii. Paul's complaint, he says, is not directed against the 'substance' (οὐσία) of the flesh or of the soul, but against their 'activity' (πρᾶξις) or 'deliberate choice' (προαίρεσις).[3] The same point is made in more directly Pauline terms by insisting that the word σάρξ in such contexts is a kind of shorthand version for the fuller phrase, 'the mind of the flesh' (τὸ φρόνημα τῆς σαρκός).[4]

This insistence that man's physical body as such is not evil is virtually universal, though not all writers make it with such vigour or clarity as Irenaeus and Tertullian. This is particularly true of their Eastern contemporary, Clement of Alexandria. He shared their anti-Gnostic concern and can insist with them that Paul does not regard the flesh as shameful;[5] it is the creation of the one God, and as such is not necessarily evil but is capable of being sanctified and brought to perfection.[6] But Clement also shared some of that same distrust of the physical which lay at the root of the Gnostic's conviction. His attitude to the Greek philosophical tradition was very far from the violent opposition of Tertullian. He is even prepared to admit a certain similarity between the attitude of Paul to the body and that of Plato.[7] The goal of life is for him to reject

---

[1] I Cor. vi. 15; iii. 16 and vi. 19; vi. 20.
[2] De Res. Mort. 10, 3–5.
[3] Chr. Hom. in Rom. 13, 2 (9, 510) on Rom. vii. 19–20. Cf. Chr. Comm. in Gal. 5, 6 (10, 673) on Gal. v. 19–22.
[4] Origen, Frag. on I Cor. v. 5 (J.T.S. IX, 364); Cyr. Al. on Rom. vii. 5 (Pusey, p. 194); Chr. Hom. in Rom. 13, 4 (9, 513) on Rom. viii. 3.
[5] Stromateis, 3, 65, 2 (Phil. i. 20–4).
[6] Ibid. 4, 26, 5; 6, 60, 2; Paidagogos, 2, 109, 3.
[7] Stromateis, 3, 18, 1–3. The Pauline text to which Clement refers is Rom. vii. 24, 'Who shall deliver me from the body of this death?' But he does express a doubt about

as far as possible all that is of man.[1] He regularly describes death as a freeing of the soul from the chains which bind it to the body, and sees it when viewed in this light as the culmination of that mutual crucifixion of self to the world and the world to self and as the full fruition of that citizenship in heaven which are the very essence of Paul's spirituality.[2] H. Seeseman points to two respects in which Clement's treatment of the body differs from that of Paul himself. In the first place Clement tends to regard the body simply as man's outer covering in a manner which is not true of Paul. Secondly, he does not draw at all the distinction which Paul normally maintains between the two terms σάρξ and σῶμα.[3] As a result his attitude towards the physical side of man's nature often seems to vacillate, in a manner more puzzling even than that of Paul himself, between one of qualified approval and of frank distrust.

But for the great majority of later writers the distinction which Irenaeus and Tertullian had drawn between a moral understanding of the concept 'flesh' and a physical or a metaphysical one provided the key which enabled them to give an interpretation of Paul's thought that was wholly free from any Gnostic tendencies. So far from increasing any apparent ambiguity on the subject which there may be in Paul's writings, they tend to eliminate it altogether. The distinction between the different senses of the word 'flesh' was something so vital to them that they tend to apply it not only in the considerable number of instances where it is clearly required by the context but also in a number of other passages of especial interest and importance where its validity is a more open question. Origen

the correct exegesis of the word 'body'; it may, he suggests, be being used figuratively to refer to the agreement of those who have been enticed into evil. This figurative sense of the word 'body' is frequently appealed to by later exegetes as a means of avoiding ascribing derogation of the body to Paul. This applies more particularly to the more difficult phrase 'body of sin'. Thus Origen, like Clement, suggests it as a possible alternative in his interpretation of Rom. vi. 6, while Chrysostom and Ambrosiaster are quite certain that the reference is entirely figurative and not to our physical body at all. (Origen, *Comm. in Rom.* 5, 9 (1045 C–1046 B); Chr. *Hom. in Rom.* 11, 1 (9, 485); Ambst. *in loc.* (101 B).)

[1] *Stromateis*, 2, 125, 5–6 (Rom. viii. 9; II Cor. x. 3; I Cor. xv. 50).

[2] *Ibid.* 4, 12, 5–6 (Gal. vi. 14; Phil. iii. 20). Cf. also *ibid.* 4, 137, 3; 5, 55, 2; 5, 106, 1; 6, 46, 3; 7, 71, 3.

[3] 'Das Paulusverständnis des Clemens Alexandrinus', *Theologische Studien und Kritiken*, CVII (1936), 327–34.

argues that the words of Rom. iii. 20 'By the works of the law shall no flesh be justified in thy sight' are to be taken as referring to those who care for the works of the flesh; it is, he says, an exact equivalent of the words of Rom. viii. 8 that 'those who are in the flesh cannot please God'. The saints, whom God foreknew, are not included, since they are not σάρξ.[1] This line of interpretation clearly weakens the apparent absoluteness of Paul's attack upon the law. Jerome, although he admits that here he is in disagreement with the majority of exegetes, refuses to interpret the 'flesh and blood' of Gal. i. 16, with which Paul did not confer, as referring to the apostles, since they were spiritual and therefore could not be designated by such a phrase.[2] When Paul says in I Cor. i. 29 that the boasting of all flesh is excluded before God, 'all flesh' is interpreted by Theodore as 'every fleshly man with his mind set on fleshly things' (πᾶς ἄνθρωπος σαρκικὸς ἐπὶ σαρκικοῖς ἔχων τὸ φρόνημα).[3] In similar vein the words of I Cor. xv. 50 that 'flesh and blood shall not inherit the kingdom of God' are regularly interpreted in a moral sense. This particular exegesis, as we shall see a little later, was supported with careful and detailed reasoning and was of fundamental importance to the understanding of Paul's resurrection doctrine.[4] This insistence on the moral significance of the term 'flesh' in Paul's writings is undoubtedly a true and important insight. But it seems clear from some of the examples just given that if it is applied too automatically and too uniformly to every occurrence of the word in his letters it can give rise to serious misinterpretation of his meaning in many cases.

But the Gnostics did not simply find in Paul the idea that the flesh is evil; they found there also their closely related belief that men are of differing but fixed natures. Paul speaks of men as χοικοί, ψυχικοί and πνευματικοί, and his use of those terms was regarded by

---

[1] Origen on Rom. iii. 20 (Scherer, p. 148; *J.T.S.* XIII, 220; *Comm. in Rom.* 3, 6—940 C).

[2] Jerome on Gal. i. 16 (326 C).

[3] Theod. on I Cor. i. 29 (Staab, p. 174). Cf. Ambst. *in loc.* (191 C).

[4] Irenaeus, *Adv. Haer.* 5, 14, 4 (Harvey, II, 362); Tertullian, *De Res. Mort.* 51, 5; *Adv. Marc.* 5, 10, 11; *ibid.* 5, 14, 4; Novatian, *De Trinitate*, 10; Chr. *Hom. in I Cor.* 42, 1 (10, 364); Ambst. *in loc.* (270 B); Pelagius *in loc.* (p. 224); Isidore, *Epp.* 1, 477. See p. 44 below.

the Valentinians as an explicit reference to the three distinct kinds of men postulated by Gnostic theory.[1] Irenaeus insists in reply that the contrasted terms refer not to different natures which are determined from the beginning of a man's life but rather to different potentialities of what man by his readiness or refusal to respond to God may become. It is clear, however, as Irenaeus fully recognizes, that Paul does use the terms to refer to classes of people and that they are related to the three parts of which man is composed.[2] The use which the Gnostics made of Paul's ideas on this score meant, therefore, that their exegesis represented a challenge to the orthodox interpreter not only on the issue of what Paul intended in his references to the flesh but also on the issue of what he intended in his references to each part of man's body. The main line of the orthodox reply is already implicit in Irenaeus' insistence that χοικοί, ψυχικοί and πνευματικοί are not fixed natures but potential forms of human existence. But the detailed implication of that insistence for Pauline exegesis as a whole had still to be worked out. The various ways in which this was done can best be seen in the work of the commentators of the Eastern Church.

According to Origen, Paul clearly teaches in I Thess. v. 23 the tripartite division of man's nature into body, soul and spirit.[3] These terms stand for the different elements in the make-up of every man, but they can also on occasion be used in accordance with the grammatical principle of synecdoche to signify man as a whole. The particular term to be used will be chosen in accordance with the context—spirit when the reference is to some nobler aspect of man's being, soul when it is to some lower aspect, flesh when it is to some worse aspect still.[4] For Origen therefore, as for the Gnostics, the three are set in a clear hierarchy of moral being and each can be used to refer to the whole man. But for Origen, unlike the Gnostics,

---

[1] Irenaeus, *Adv. Haer.* 1, 8, 3 (Harvey, 1, 72) (I Cor. xv. 48; ii. 14; ii. 15).

[2] *Ibid.* 5, 8, 3–5, 9, 3 (Harvey, 11, 341–4).

[3] Origen, *Comm. in Rom.* 1, 10 (836 A) on Rom. i. 9; *Dial. Herac.* ed. Scherer, p. 136.

[4] Origen, *Comm. in Rom.* 9, 25 (1226 A, B) on Rom. xiii. 1. Cf. Jerome on Gal. vi. 18 (438 B) and on Philemon 25 (618 B). Pelagius also emphasizes that the use of the part for the whole is a regular scriptural custom of importance for the understanding of this aspect of Paul's thought (Pelagius on Rom. viii. 5, p. 62; on I Cor. v. 5, p. 152).

all three elements are to be found in every man and no one is by virtue of his creation exclusively and permanently of one particular character.

The word 'spirit' does not always have precisely the same significance. But Origen is quite clear that there are a number of Pauline texts (in addition to I Thess. v. 23) where it must refer to the human spirit, a fundamental component of man's being. His favourite examples are Rom. viii. 16 and I Cor. ii. 11.[1] The 'spirit' in such contexts is the good element in man, incapable of evil. Only once in the whole of Scripture can he find it used in a bad sense.[2] But 'spirit' may also be used to refer to the Holy Spirit. Such references, Origen believes, are normally characterized by the absence of the article or other qualifying term.[3] But he is not anxious to draw the distinction too sharply. The fruit of the spirit in Gal. v. 22 he understands sometimes of the Holy Spirit and sometimes of man's spirit.[4] The spirit is the good element in man standing in opposition to the flesh, but it still needs the help and instruction of the Holy Spirit. The aim of the Christian life is not the separation but the union of the two.

In direct opposition and contrast to the spirit stands the flesh. It is an opposing element within man himself weakening and fighting against the good intentions of the spirit. Origen was a successor to Clement at Alexandria and shared something of his approach. He is quite explicit in argument with Celsus that matter as such is not evil,[5] but he takes very seriously the fact that this downward pull within man is called 'flesh'. He quotes Gal. v. 17 as evidence that some sins 'do not proceed from the opposing powers but take their beginnings from the natural movements of the body'.[6] Such a statement is obviously very close to that fundamentally dualistic interpretation of Paul which the anti-Gnostic writers so

---

[1] Origen, *Comm. in Rom.* 2, 9 (893 B, C) on Rom. ii. 15; *Dial. Herac.* ed. Scherer, p. 136; Jerome on Gal. iii. 2 (349 D–350 A) and on Eph. iv. 4 (495 C).

[2] *Comm. in Joann.* 32, 18 (the reference is to Deut. ii. 30).

[3] *De Principiis*, 1, 3, 4 (where Origen attributes the idea to his predecessors); Jerome on Gal. v. 18 (413 C).

[4] *De Principiis*, 1, 3, 4; *in Luc.* Fr. 112 (of the Holy Spirit); *Comm. in Joann.* 32, 18; Jerome on Gal. v. 22 (419 A) (of man's spirit).

[5] *Con. Cel.* 3, 42; 4, 66.

[6] *De Principiis*, 3, 2, 3.

vigorously repudiate. Origen's interpretation is to be distinguished from such a complete dualism by his insistence that this struggle between flesh and spirit falls within and not outside the orbit of God's providence.[1] Our physical existence is not a part of God's original and basic creation, but rather a punishment for the fall of the pre-existent soul. In this way Origen seeks to do justice to the dualistic element to be found both in human experience and in the writings of Paul without having recourse to a full metaphysical dualism. Such ideas arise naturally in the course of his speculative rather than directly exegetical work. In so far as they could claim to have an origin in the thought of Paul, that origin might be found in Paul's conception of the whole creation as subjected to vanity; Origen interprets that vanity as bodily existence. Paul's words describe exactly Origen's understanding of the role of the body—it is vanity and a cause of groaning, but it is also in accordance with the will of God and in hope of a future glorious redemption.[2]

Thus Origen's thought about the nature of man tends, like that of Paul, to find expression in bipolar terms—as a union of the conflicting elements of flesh and spirit. Sometimes indeed he adopts the Pauline language of an inner and outer man, and identifies these with soul and body.[3] Nevertheless this tendency seems to have been exaggerated by Rufinus, who is inclined to misrepresent Origen's teaching on occasions by giving it in a twofold instead of in a threefold form.[4] Certainly Origen more often adheres, especially in the work of exegesis, to the tripartite division of body, soul and spirit. But both patterns of thought do clearly go back to Origen and both are significantly linked by him with the teaching of Paul himself.[5] Origen does not however find it easy to give clear expression to the precise nature and function of the soul.[6] It is distinct

[1] Cf. Owen Chadwick, *John Cassian* (1950), p. 89, which speaks of 'the tradition of Origen that the war of flesh and spirit, found in every man and therefore a creation of God and therefore good, benefits humanity'.

[2] *De Principiis*, 1, 7, 5; *Con. Cel.* 7, 50 (Rom. viii. 20–3).

[3] Origen, *Comm. in Can. Cantic.* Prolog. (*G.C.S.* ed. Baehrens, p. 64); *Con. Cel.* 7, 38 (Rom. vii. 22; II Cor. iv. 16).

[4] Cf. K. H. Schelkle, *Paulus Lehrer der Väter*, p. 218.

[5] Cf. H. de Lubac, *Histoire et Esprit* (1950), pp. 156–7.

[6] There is of course a parallel here to Origen's treatment of the various senses of Scripture. Formally he asserts that there are three—body, soul and spirit—but the

from the spirit, which may need to be roused but cannot sink to the point of death,[1] and in the judgement on the wicked the two may be completely separated.[2] It stands, he says, in a mid-way position between the weak flesh and the willing spirit, capable of turning either to good or to evil.[3] Yet it is not an entirely neutral concept morally. It may not have the strong downward pull of the flesh, yet it is normally spoken of in Scripture in terms not of praise but of censure.[4] Origen's view, in so far as it can be determined with any certainty, seems to be that it is that part of man which has fallen away from its original status, but which is capable of restoration through association with the spirit.[5] Thus the soul like the flesh is evil, but less radically so; but again as in the case of the body that element of evil does not involve any belief either in evil as the direct creation of God or in some rival creative evil power.[6]

But in the work of Pauline exegesis it is the destiny of the soul rather than its origin which is of importance. The normal situation in man is 'a disastrous friendship of soul and body'; this must be broken and the soul must associate itself completely with the spirit in its struggle against the flesh.[7] Origen does envisage the possibility of the soul's maintaining its own independence, siding neither with the flesh nor with the spirit, but he regards this as an even worse situation than its association with the flesh. He gives two reasons for this rather surprising judgement. In the first place there is more likelihood of repugnance from the sins of the flesh and therefore a greater possibility of conversion; and in the second place this intermediate position is no better than that of an irrational animal.[8] But the all-important thing is the possibility and the great

distinction between soul and spirit is a somewhat unsatisfactory one, and in practice Origen often works in terms of two rather than three senses.

[1] Origen, Frag. on Eph. v. 14 (*J.T.S.* III, 563). The first half of the words 'Awake thou that sleepest and arise from the dead' are to be understood as referring to the spirit, the second half as referring to the soul.

[2] Origen, *Comm. in Rom.* 2, 9 (893 C) on Rom. ii. 15. Cf. *Matt. Comm. Ser.* 62; *De Principiis*, 2, 10, 7.

[3] *De Principiis*, 2, 8, 4; *Comm. in Joann.* 32, 18.

[4] *De Princiipis*, 2, 8, 3.

[5] *Ibid.* 2, 8, 2.

[6] *Hom. in Can. Cantic.* 2, 1 (*G.C.S.* ed. Baehrens, p. 42).

[7] *Comm. in Joann.* 1, 32.   [8] *De Principiis*, 3, 4, 3.

benefits of the soul's self-identification with the spirit. That which is ψυχικός is not automatically and eternally so by nature; it can become πνευματικός.[1] The effect of receiving the Holy Spirit is first of all to make holy the spirit that is in man. This effect can then be passed on to the soul.[2] For 'that which is joined to the spirit is spirit' and it is the privilege and destiny of the soul to be so joined to the spirit that it ceases to be soul and becomes what the spirit is.[3]

The distinction which Origen had drawn between those references to 'spirit' in the Bible which referred to the human spirit and those which referred to the Holy Spirit became a matter of increasing significance in the fourth century as a result of the growing interest in the question of the divine nature of the Holy Spirit. One of the arguments which Athanasius uses in his letters to Serapion is the claim that his opponents falsely assume that every scriptural reference to 'spirit' is to be understood of the Holy Spirit. In combating their argument Athanasius quotes Origen's familiar examples—Rom. viii. 16, I Cor. ii. 11 and I Thess. v. 23—as cases where the reference cannot be to the Holy Spirit.[4] For the purposes of his argument Athanasius is concerned to reduce the number of occasions which may be allowed to be direct references to the Holy Spirit to those which speak unmistakably of his divinity. He therefore argues (this time in direct contrast to Origen) that references to 'spirit' should be understood of the Holy Spirit only if the article is used or some other qualifying phrase.[5]

One outcome of this anxiety that scriptural texts employing the word 'spirit' might be used as evidence against the affirmation of the

[1] Origen, Frag. on I Cor. ii. 14 (*J.T.S.* ix, 240). Cf. Isidore (*Epp.* 4, 81), who makes this point by emphasizing that the text reads οὐ δέχεται and not οὐ δέξεται.

[2] Origen, Frag. on Eph. iv. 30 (*J.T.S.* iii, 556).

[3] Origen, Frag. on I Cor. vii. 28 (*J.T.S.* ix, 510); on Rom. vi. 12 (*J.T.S.* xiii, 365–6); *De Oratione*, 9, 2; Jerome on Gal. v. 17, v. 19–21 and Philemon 25 (411 B; 415 A, B; 618 B) (I Cor. vi. 17). Cf. H. Crouzel, *Théologie de l'image de Dieu chez Origène* (1956), p. 133. Victorinus in his commentary on Ephesians sets out the idea of the transformation of 'anima' into 'spiritus' as the basic expression there of God's purpose for mankind (on Eph. i. 4, i. 8 and i. 23—1239–41; 1244; 1252). Indeed he interprets both the 'making both one' of Eph. ii. 15 and the unity of man and wife of Eph. v. 32 in terms of this union of soul and spirit (1258 D–1259 A, 1289 B). Cf. also Pelagius on Gal. v. 16 (p. 335).

[4] Athanasius, *Ep. ad Ser.* 1, 4.

[5] *Ibid.* 1, 7.

full divinity of the Holy Spirit was to increase the proportion of references to 'spirit' which the orthodox interpreter of Paul was inclined to apply to the human spirit. We can see this result reflected in the writings of Didymus. He follows Origen, but with greater emphasis, in accepting a threefold division of man's nature. I Thess. v. 23, he insists, must be interpreted in that way; it would be absurd or rather blasphemous to interpret 'spirit' in Paul's prayer as referring to the Holy Spirit, which is necessarily perfect.[1] In that text 'soul' and 'spirit' are clearly distinct from one another. Similarly when I Cor. ii. 11 speaks of the spirit of man knowing the things of a man, it cannot simply be bodily facts that the spirit knows; there must therefore be a distinction between the soul, which is known, and the spirit, which knows. But the two words are not always so to be distinguished in the Pauline writings; sometimes 'spirit' is used as a simple equivalent for 'soul'.[2] Thus, whether as a distinct part of man or as an alternative name for the soul, the bulk of the occurrences of the term 'spirit' in Paul's writings are references to a natural element in man's make-up. Didymus is as clear and as emphatic as Athanasius had been that where the reference is to the Holy Spirit it is clearly indicated by the use of the article or other qualifying phrase.[3] He is well aware, however, that there were others who argued the case the other way round. Some people, he says, insist that where πνεῦμα stands without qualification it *must* refer to the Holy Spirit; only if some qualifying words are expressly stated should it be understood of the human spirit. II Cor. vii. 1, with its call to a cleansing 'from every defilement of body and spirit', is an obvious difficulty for such a view. To Didymus the text presents no problem, and he treats 'spirit' here as equivalent in meaning to 'soul'. But those who insisted that unqualified references to πνεῦμα must refer to the Holy Spirit were forced in this instance to adopt the harsh expedient of placing a comma after σαρκός instead of after πνεύματος and construing the sentence to mean 'let us

---

[1] Didymus, *De Spiritu Sancto*, 55 (*P.G.* 39, 1080 B).

[2] *Ibid.* 54 (*P.G.* 39, 1079 C, D). The examples which he gives there of spirit as an equivalent to soul are all non-Pauline, e.g. Jas. ii. 26, Acts vii. 38, Eccl. iii. 21. But see his interpretation of II Cor. vii. 1 below.

[3] *De Trinitate*, 2 (*P.G.* 39, 457 C); *De Spiritu Sancto*, 3 and 15 (*P.G.* 39, 1035 A, 1048 A).

cleanse ourselves from every defilement of the body, so perfecting the holiness of the Spirit in the fear of God'.[1]

The Antiochenes were as anxious as Didymus was to safeguard the full divinity of the Holy Spirit, but that concern did not lead them in the same direction in their interpretation of Pauline references to 'spirit'. Severian gives the strongest expression to the principle which guided their exegesis. Not only, in his view, should πνεῦμα not be taken to refer to man's spirit unless explicit indication to that effect is given; it should never be understood as a natural element in man at all. By nature man consists of body and soul; it is only the believer and never the unbeliever who can be described in threefold terms as body, soul and spirit.[2] Spirit is never a natural element in man, but that does not imply that all references to spirit are references to the divine person of the Holy Spirit himself. The greater part are references to the gift (χάρισμα) of the Holy Spirit imparted to men. All the Antiochenes interpret 'spirit' in I Thess. v. 23 in this way. Severian seeks to meet the objection of Didymus to such an interpretation by pointing out that Paul's prayer is that they may be kept ἀμέμπτως not ἄμεμπτα; that is to say it is not the quality of the thing given but our use of it that Paul is praying about.[3] So too Diodore and Chrysostom interpret the 'our spirit' of Rom. viii. 16 with which the Spirit bears witness as 'that which we have through baptism'.[4] The general position adopted is well summed up in Isidore's description of the threefold classification of men into πνευματικός, ψυχικός and σαρκικός. In each case man is named after the dominant component in his make-up, but the three are not precisely parallel. The πνευματικός has a body and a soul in addition to the ruling spirit; the ψυχικός and the σαρκικός on the other hand have only one other component each in addition to the dominant one after which they are named; neither has a spirit at all.[5]

---

[1] Didymus on II Cor. vii. 1 (Staab, pp. 32–3). This punctuation and interpretation of the text is followed by Ambrosiaster on II Cor. vii. 1 (303 A). Augustine argues that the text is ambiguous, and that since both renderings give an orthodox sense the issue may be left to the judgement of the reader (*De Doctrina Christiana*, 3, 11, 5).

[2] Severian on I Thess. v. 23 (Staab, p. 331).

[3] Severian, *loc. cit.*; Theod. *in loc.* (Swete, II, 39); Chr. *Hom. in I Thess.* 11, 2 (11, 463). This is also the interpretation of Ambrosiaster (454 A) and Pelagius (p. 437).

[4] Diodore on Rom. viii. 16 (Staab, pp. 92–3); Chr. *Hom. in Rom.* 14, 3 (9, 527).

[5] Isidore, *Epp.* 4, 127 (I Cor. ii. 14).

At first sight Theodore of Mopsuestia, the greatest of all the Antiochene exegetes, seems to provide a partial exception to this general rule. He does admit that πνεῦμα may be used on occasion as a synonym for 'mind' (διάνοια) or 'will' (πρόθεσις). He allows this as a possibility in the case of Rom. i. 9, though it is not the interpretation which he himself prefers; in Rom. ii. 29, where he does interpret the word in that way, he points out in so doing that the whole context is concerned with the sphere of natural law and not with that of grace at all.[1] In such a context it could hardly be interpreted as the special gift of the Holy Spirit. But the exception is more apparent than real. Theodore is simply claiming that πνεῦμα is sometimes used as a synonym for some other part of man's inner make-up. There is no real deviation from the underlying Antiochene conviction that in his basic created nature man must be understood to consist simply of body and soul. It is questionable whether this elimination of 'spirit' from man's ordinary created nature is wholly true to the detailed form in which Paul expresses himself. But Paul's thought does so frequently follow a bipolar form that those who, like the Antiochenes, thought more exclusively in such terms were not likely to be led badly astray by that fact in their interpretation of his teaching.

In his basic approach, therefore, Theodore does not really stand out as different from the other Antiochenes. The point at which his exegesis is most distinctive and of greatest interest is in his understanding of the concept 'flesh'. Paul, he says, does use the word to describe the natural, physical part of man, but it has also another far more significant usage whereby it stands for mortality and the transitoriness of life.[2] It is the fact of mortality which inevitably leads us into sin. The soul, thanks to the law, is capable of recognizing and desiring the good, but it is not strong enough to combat the sin that arises from our mortality.[3] When Paul declares that 'in

---

[1] Theod. on Rom. i. 9 (Staab, p. 114); on Rom. ii. 29 (Staab, p. 116).

[2] Theod. on Rom. vii. 5 (Staab, pp. 124–5). Cf. also on Rom. xiii. 14 (Staab, p. 164); on II Cor. x. 3–4 (Staab, p. 199); on Gal. ii. 20 (Swete, I, 35); on Gal. iii. 3 (Swete, I, 37); on Gal. iv. 29 (Swete, I, 85); on Gal. v. 13 (Swete, I, 94); on Gal. v. 16 (Swete, I, 98); on Gal. v. 19–21 (Swete, I, 99); on Philemon 16 (Swete, II, 282).

[3] Theod. on Rom. vii. 19–20, 21, 25 (Staab, pp. 131–2, 132, 133). With Theodore's comment on Rom. vii. 25 ὑπὸ τῆς θνητότητος ἐπὶ τὴν ἁμαρτίαν καθέλκομαι contrast

me that is in my flesh dwells no good thing' it is to the power of mortality to produce sin that he refers; the achievement of virtue requires us to reason and to act *sub specie aeternitatis*, and this our mortality will not let us do.[1] The mind of the flesh is the mind that thinks in terms of the present world only. Man's predicament therefore is a struggle between, on the one hand, the flesh or mortality, and on the other the 'mind of the soul' (τὸ φρόνημα τῆς ψυχῆς) in which any natural goodness there may be resides.[2] This conflict is resolved by the coming of the Spirit. Since the root of man's trouble is his mortality, then the Spirit, which is the spirit of life, takes away mortality and thereby takes away the source of the conflict and restores peace to man.[3] Thus the Spirit is never natural to man; it is the source of immortality,[4] and it is to this fundamental characteristic of it that Paul refers when he speaks of it as the spirit of life,[5] or as the spirit of promise[6] or when he speaks of 'spiritual blessings in heavenly places'.[7] There is one development of particular interest which Theodore gives to this conception of man as compounded of body and soul, and of his predicament as being a conflict between the two. As body, man is linked to the natural world, as soul, to the invisible powers. The proper link between the two has been broken in man and this has resulted in a breaking of harmonious relationship in the universe as a whole. Man by his dual nature constitutes the essential link, and so it is only as harmony is restored within man himself that true harmony will be restored in the universe at large.[8]

---

that of Diodore on Rom. vii. 24 τοῦ κατέχοντος τὸ σῶμα θανάτου διὰ τῆς ἁμαρτίας (Staab, p. 90). Isidore also insists that for Paul the root problem is sin and not death (*Epp.* 4, 52). The emphasis in Theodore's teaching that mortality is a cause of sin is not exclusive of the apparently opposite teaching that sin is a cause of mortality (see U. Wickert, *Studien zu den Pauluskommentaren Theodors von Mopsuestia* (1962), p. 115; R. A. Norris, *Manhood and Christ* (1963), p. 184).

[1] Theod. on Rom. vii. 18 (Staab, p. 131).
[2] Theod. on Rom. viii. 5–6 (Staab, p. 135).   [3] *Ibid.*
[4] Theod. on Gal. iii. 2–3 (Swete, I, 37); on Gal. v. 16 (Swete, I, 98); on Gal. vi. 18 (Swete, I, 110–11); on I Thess. iv. 9 (Swete, II, 25).
[5] Theod. on Rom. viii. 2 (Staab, p. 133).
[6] Theod. on Eph. i. 14 (Swete, I, 132–3).
[7] Theod. on Eph. i. 3 (Swete, I, 122).
[8] Theod. on Rom. viii. 19 (Staab, pp. 137–8); on Col. i. 16 (Swete, I, 267–9). Theodore interprets this latter verse in terms not of the original creation but of the final summing up of all things in Christ (see p. 79 below).

The understanding of the idea of flesh in the Western commentators has interesting affinities with that of Theodore. They do not go as far as he does in seeing the mere fact of mortality as the meaning of 'flesh' and the root cause of man's trouble. But they do understand the term as implying an exclusive concern for this present world. Irenaeus had interpreted Paul's words that flesh and blood could not inherit the kingdom of heaven as referring to those who live as if they were flesh and blood and nothing more.[1] Ambrosiaster is most emphatic about the variety of meanings that the term bears in Paul's writing. In addition to the obvious senses of man's physical body and of man in his sinfulness, he claims that it is sometimes exactly equivalent to 'mundus', and he understands the mind of the flesh as a refusal to believe the supernatural; it is the mind which accepts only the realm of this world.[2] Augustine's understanding of the idea is similar but is focused upon the will rather than the intellect. For him the mind of the flesh is the mind whose choices are determined by the desire for purely temporal good and the fear of purely temporal evil.[3]

The one thing that unites all orthodox interpreters of Paul's anthropological language is their convinced rejection of all radically dualistic or deterministic interpretations of his words. Indeed it is primarily that fact which constitutes them orthodox interpreters. Even though we have only been able to sketch the nature of their interpretation in the barest outline, we have seen enough to recognize that within that common bond of agreement there was scope for wide variations of emphasis. The general nature of that variation can best be illustrated by comparing two of the greatest figures of the period, Origen and Chrysostom. Some account has already been given of the general character of Origen's exegesis. Chrysostom follows the main lines of Antiochene thought. He accepts the dual analysis of man's nature. His interpretation of such texts as I Thess. v. 23, Rom. viii. 16 and Rom. i. 9 shows that he regards πνεῦμα as an additional gift to the Christian rather than as a natural

[1] Irenaeus, *Adv. Haer.* 5, 9, 4 (Harvey, II, 345) (I Cor. xv. 50).
[2] Ambst. on Rom. vi. 8; vii. 5; viii. 5–6; I Cor. i. 29; Gal. v. 24 (101 B, C, 107 B, C, 119 A, B, 191 C, 368 C, D).
[3] Aug. *Expos. Prop. Ep. ad Rom.* 48 (Rom. viii. 3–4); *ibid.* 49 (Rom. viii. 7).

element in human life.[1] Flesh and soul are both morally neutral; there is nothing wrong with either of them as such; the evil lies not in their nature but in their abuse.[2] Being comparatively unconcerned with the philosophical question of the origin of evil, he is able to make this point far more directly and definitely than Origen. Flesh and soul are the good creations of God, and difficulty only arises if they try to exceed their appointed station. As a homilist, Chrysostom's primary concern is not with man's nature as it has been or as it is, but as in Christian life it is meant to be. This he depicts in terms of a hierarchy of subordination. The flesh is the chariot, the soul the charioteer and the imparted spirit comes in at the head of the hierarchy as the charioteer's skill.[3] It is the breaking of this harmonious order that gives rise to sin. Sometimes, as in the case of incest at Corinth, it is the flesh that has issued the commands and given rise to the sin; in such a case therefore it is, as Paul decrees, the flesh that must suffer.[4] But far more often the flesh is only acting in its rightful subordination to the soul, and the responsibility must therefore be laid at the door of the soul rather than of the flesh. It is the workman rather than the tool which is to be blamed.[5] Where Origen emphasizes the flesh as the primary power for evil in human life, Chrysostom lays the main emphasis on the failings of the soul.[6] For these two reasons therefore—his comparative lack of interest in ultimate philosophical questions and his stress on the greater responsibility of the soul as senior partner in that organic union which is man—Chrysostom is able to give a much more

---

[1] Chr. *Hom. in I Thess.* 11, 2 (11, 463); *Hom. in Rom.* 14, 3 (9, 527); *Hom. in Rom.* 2, 2 (9, 402).

[2] Chr. *Hom. in Rom.* 13, 7 (9, 518) on Rom. viii. 9.

[3] Chr. *Hom. in Rom.* 13, 6 (9, 516) on Rom. viii. 5–7; *Hom. in I Cor.* 7, 4 (10, 60) on I Cor. ii. 14; *Hom. in Eph.* 5, 4 (11, 41) on Eph. ii. 16.

[4] Chr. *Hom. in I Cor.* 15, 2 (10, 124) on I Cor. v. 5.

[5] Chr. *Hom. in Rom.* 11, 3 (9, 487) on Rom. vi. 13; *ibid.* 12, 3 (9, 498) on Rom. vii. 5; *ibid.* 13, 2 (9, 509) on Rom. vii. 17–18; *ibid.* 13, 3 (9, 511) on Rom. vii. 23.

[6] The division here is certainly not to be regarded as one between Alexandria and Antioch. On this issue Diodore sides with Origen and Didymus with Chrysostom (Diodore on Rom. vii. 22–3—Staab, p. 89; Didymus on Rom. vii. 20—Staab, pp. 5–6). Ambrosiaster asserts that it is the soul which was primarily responsible for Adam's sin, but that it is the body which is corrupted thereby and by which inherited sin is passed on (Ambst. on Rom. vii. 18 and 22—113A, 114A).

positive evaluation to the role of the body in human life than Origen does.

This difference of emphasis is reflected in their differing handling of the term σάρξ. For Chrysostom there are two clearly distinct uses of the term. The one is morally neutral and refers to the physical body; the other, which is equivalent to the fuller phrase 'the mind of the flesh' (τὸ φρόνημα τῆς σαρκός), is necessarily bad but its link with the physical body is left unemphasized and unexplained.[1] He feels free to choose between these two senses and to apply one exclusively of the other on any particular occasion. Origen, on the other hand, seeks as far as possible to give a uniform interpretation to the word σάρξ throughout his interpretation of Paul. Its meaning is not simply physical substance as such; it does imply 'the mind of the flesh', as the inclusion of heresy among the works of the flesh bears out.[2] But even in such contexts a connection with the physical body is not entirely absent; it is not identical with the physical body, but it always remains far more closely connected with it than it does for Chrysostom. Thus for Origen the word σάρξ can never be entirely freed from its depreciatory significance.

The same point can be given further illustration by two examples of places where their exegesis of Paul diverges on this issue. Origen, as we have seen, interprets the 'groaning' of which Paul speaks in Rom. viii as the frustration which is endemic to bodily existence. Chrysostom, however, insists that the concept implies no disparagement of our present lot; it is expressive simply of our longing for the unspeakable joys of ultimate redemption, of whose wonder we are assured by our present experience of their first-fruits.[3] Our second example is from the account of Paul's subduing of his body in I Cor. ix. 26-7. Chrysostom insists that the enemy against whom Paul is fighting is not the flesh but the devil; the flesh is no enemy and therefore Paul does not speak of killing it, but only of

---

[1] Chr. *Hom. in Rom.* 13, 7 (9, 518) on Rom. viii. 9. Tertullian, who emphasizes the responsibility of the soul as against the flesh in human sin even more strongly than Chrysostom, had asserted that φρόνημα τῆς σαρκός was to be referred to the soul (*De Res. Mort.* 46, 13).

[2] Origen, Frag. on Rom. vi. 12 (*J.T.S.* XIII, 331; *Comm. in Rom.* 6, 1—1055 C). The same argument occurs in Ambrosiaster on Gal. v. 24 (368 D).

[3] Chr. *Hom. in Rom.* 14, 6 (9, 531) on Rom. viii. 23.

bringing it into subjection, that is to say restoring it to its rightful place as a servant.[1] On both scores Origen is directly opposed to him, and is fully prepared to use the stronger terms of man's fight against the flesh. With reference to the same verses (I Cor. ix. 26–7) he insists that the flesh is a most formidable enemy and is to be treated as such, so that the soul may be freed from its blandishments and truly united with the spirit.[2] When God declares 'I kill and I make alive', it is a killing of the flesh and a making alive of the spirit of which he speaks.[3] Paul himself clearly uses both kinds of language; he speaks sometimes of the subordination, sometimes of the mortification of the flesh. The two ideas, even if at first sight formally incompatible, are not irreconcilably so. Yet they do represent a real difference of emphasis, and the fact that it is the one picture which is taken up and developed by Chrysostom and the other which is taken up and developed by Origen is symptomatic of a real difference of emphasis between them.

But this difference of emphasis has its clearest and most important manifestation in their differing treatments of the subject of man's destiny. Where Origen speaks of the freeing of the soul from its association with the flesh and restoring it to its true association with the spirit, for Chrysostom soul and flesh stand much more on an equal footing. As the rebellions of flesh and soul are fundamentally the same in kind, so they can in equal manner be restored to their rightful place in God's purpose. The whole man (body and soul alike) thereby becomes spiritual or more simply spirit, even though still having a physical body. The only distinction between body and soul in this account of their restoration is that the soul's rightful place in the hierarchy is superior to that of the body, and it can therefore be spoken of as sharing in the Spirit's rule. But the distinction is far less important than the fundamental similarity; both body and soul are equally capable of entering into salvation and both can do so only by the one means of subordination to the

---

[1] Chr. *Hom. in I Cor.* 23, 1–2 (10, 189–90).

[2] Origen, *Comm. in Rom.* 7, 12 (1136 C–1137 A) on Rom. viii. 38–9. In commenting on the great list of adversaries which Paul is confident cannot separate him from the love of God, Origen points out that he does not include 'flesh' in the list; this, he suggests, is because Paul always remained afraid of its power against him.

[3] Origen, *Hom. in Lev.* 3, 4 (Deut. xxxii. 39).

Spirit.[1] This difference about the place of the body in the salvation of man comes to its climax in differing accounts of the resurrection of the body.

On this issue Chrysostom stands clearly in the main line of traditional orthodoxy, which proclaimed the resuscitation of this physical body and its entry into eternal life. Modern Christian thought is inclined to feel scant sympathy for this belief, and it is important therefore to notice at the outset that it cannot be treated as if it were the unfortunate but comparatively isolated incursion of a piece of crude materialism into the thought of the Fathers; as the foregoing discussion has made clear, it was integrated into the very fabric of their thought and represented for them the crown and climax of the Christian's distinctively positive approach towards the physical creation. This is true not only of Chrysostom but equally of Irenaeus, who was the first to give clear development to this belief and to ground it, in part at least, upon the writings of Paul.

Irenaeus employs four main lines of argument in showing that the resurrection of the physical body is the intended teaching of Paul. First of all he quotes the prayer of Paul in his letter to the Thessalonians that their 'spirit, soul and body may be preserved blameless until the coming of the Lord Jesus Christ'. Such a prayer, he argues, would have no point unless all the three elements were to have a part in that ultimate salvation which the coming of the Lord inaugurates.[2] Secondly, he argues that the language which Paul uses about 'raising up', 'putting on immortality', and 'mortality being swallowed up by life' is only applicable to the flesh. Neither soul nor spirit is mortal and such language must therefore necessarily refer to the flesh.[3] Thirdly, he argues from Paul's description of present Christian experience. Christians, while still having their physical bodies, can be 'in the spirit' and receive 'the Spirit of God whereby

---

[1] Chr. *Hom. in Rom.* 13, 7–8 (9, 518) on Rom. viii. 9; *Hom. in I Cor.* 18, 3 (10, 148) on I Cor. vi. 17.

[2] Irenaeus, *Adv. Haer.* 5, 6, 1 (Harvey, II, 335) (I Thess. v. 23). Cf. Victorinus on Phil. iv. 7, where he reads 'the peace of God will keep your hearts and your *bodies*' (instead of 'thoughts') and develops the same argument from that reading (1230A).

[3] Irenaeus, *Adv. Haer.* 5, 7, 1 (Harvey, II, 336–7) (Rom. viii. 11); *ibid.* 5, 13, 3 (Harvey, II, 357) (I Cor. xv. 53; II Cor. v. 4). Cf. Pelagius on I Cor. xv. 14 (pp. 215–16).

we cry Abba Father'; fleshly tables of the heart can be inscribed upon by the Spirit of the living God. The presence of the Spirit now to a degree which entitles men to be described as spiritual is not incompatible with fleshly existence; nor therefore need it be so in the life of the resurrection.[1] Finally, he appeals to the means by which Christ has won our redemption. It is by the *blood* of Christ that those who were afar off have been brought near; it is in his *flesh* that Christ has abolished the commandments that were against us; it is in the *flesh* that Christ has risen. Christ would not have needed to use flesh and blood as the means of our redemption were our flesh and blood not to be redeemed.[2]

Over against this, he says, the heretics' case is built upon a single verse—I Cor. xv. 50, 'Flesh and blood cannot inherit the kingdom of God.' We have already noted the main way in which this objection was met. Irenaeus in fact uses three lines of argument. In the first instance the words are defined to mean that flesh and blood by themselves, apart from the Spirit, cannot enter the kingdom of God.[3] Secondly, flesh and blood are defined as not bearing their straightforward meaning but as implying the works of the flesh, and Gal. v. 19–21 is cited in evidence.[4] These two lines of argument may be said to be brought together in the declaration already quoted that Paul's meaning is that if you live as if you were flesh and blood and nothing more you cannot inherit the kingdom of God.[5] Thirdly, though he clearly lays much less emphasis on this line of argument, it would be incorrect in any sense to speak of flesh and blood inheriting the kingdom; the relationship is the other way round; it is they that are inherited.[6]

All these arguments recur with great frequency in later writers.

---

[1] Irenaeus, *Adv. Haer.* 5, 8, 1 (Harvey, II, 339) (Rom. viii. 9 and 15); *ibid.* 5, 13, 4 (Harvey, II, 358) (II Cor. iii. 3).

[2] *Ibid.* 5, 14, 3 (Harvey, II, 362) (Eph. ii. 13 and 15); *ibid.* 5, 7, 1 (Harvey, II, 336).

[3] *Ibid.* 5, 9, 1–3 (Harvey, II, 341–4).

[4] *Ibid.* 5, 11, 1; 5, 14, 4 (Harvey, II, 347–8, 362–3).

[5] *Ibid.* 5, 9, 4 (Harvey, II, 344–5) (see p. 39 above). This shows the way in which Irenaeus relates the two primary Pauline senses of flesh without implying any derogation of the physical creation as such.

[6] *Ibid.* Cf. Methodius on I Cor. xv. 50 (Cramer, p. 329); *De Res.* 2, 18, 9, where the interpretation is attributed to Justin.

THE NATURE OF MAN

They lie behind Chrysostom's exegesis of the relevant Pauline passages, and there is no need to illustrate them again from his writings. On only one issue is there a significant difference. Chrysostom is very cautious in his use of the argument from Christian experience. It is one which might seem to fit very naturally into his thought; but if the argument be used to substantiate the basic fact of a physical resurrection, then it would inevitably tend to imply that only those who were in Christ would enjoy a resurrection of the body. It is an essential element in Chrysostom's thought that *all* will rise again, and he sees this idea implied in many Pauline texts. If Paul speaks of the presence of the Spirit in our hearts as an assurance that 'he who raised up Christ Jesus from the dead shall quicken also your mortal bodies', he has deliberately used the word 'quicken' (ζωοποιήσει) and not 'raise up' (ἀναστήσει) to show that he is referring not simply to the resurrection of the body but rather to the gift of eternal life.[1] So, on the other hand, when Paul writes that 'as in Adam all die even so in Christ shall all be made alive', he is referring only to the resurrection of the body. This exegesis, it will be noticed, weakens the emphasis that he lays on Paul's choice of the word ζωοποιεῖν in Rom. viii. 11.[2] The 'all' who must stand before the judgement seat of Christ must assuredly include sinners;[3] it is they who are referred to as being clothed and yet found naked,[4] and Paul's reference to the two distinct kinds of body—heavenly and earthly—in his discussion of the resurrection of the body has the same implication.[5]

Thus the resurrection of the body is understood to be an essential element in salvation, though in two respects it is not to be

[1] Chr. *Hom. in Rom.* 13, 8 (9, 519–20) on Rom. viii. 11. Cf. *Hom. in Phil.* 11, 3 (11, 267) on Phil. iii. 11.
[2] Chr. *Hom. in I Cor.* 39, 3 (10, 336–7) on I Cor. xv. 22. The same point had been made by Origen. 'All died in Adam'—including the righteous Abraham, Isaac, Jacob, etc.; 'all will rise in Christ'—including the unrighteous; but it will be 'each in his own order' (Frag. on I Cor. xv. 22–3—*J.T.S.* x, 48). Cf. also Ambst. *in loc.* (264 A). Pelagius gives a different exegesis which preserves Chrysostom's suggestion that ζωοποιεῖν has a deeper meaning; it is true, he says, that all rise, but the point here made is that it is only 'all who are in Christ' who will be made alive (Pelagius *in loc.* p. 217). [3] Chr. *Hom. in II Cor.* 10, 3 (10, 470) on II Cor. v. 10.
[4] Chr. *Hom. in II Cor.* 10, 1 (10, 467) on II Cor. v. 3; *De Res. Mort.* 8.
[5] Chr. *Hom. in I Cor.* 41, 3 (10, 358) on I Cor. xv. 40.

identified with that salvation. In the first place resurrection of the
body will be the common experience of the righteous and of sinners
alike; to the righteous will be added the gift of life in the fullest
meaning of that word. In the second place the resurrection of the
body is not to be understood as the mere continuance of the life of
the flesh. The body will be the same in 'substance' (οὐσία) but
better in 'quality of appearance' (εὐπρέπεια);[1] it will no longer be a
body of humiliation but will have been transformed by the gift of
'incorruption' (ἀφθαρσία);[2] it will be a πνευματικός body, which may
mean simply that it will be perfectly controlled by the Spirit, but
which may also be understood to mean that without any change of
'nature' (φύσις) it will yet acquire new qualities of physical light-
ness, surpassing in beauty even those known to us in the heavenly
bodies.[3]

The idea of the spiritual body, therefore, was understood within
the main line of orthodox thought to have a threefold meaning.
In the first place it had a moral sense and implied such perfect inte-
gration with the spirit as to constitute a complete release from all
that is signified by 'the mind of the flesh'.[4] Secondly, it involved, as
even Tertullian readily admitted, a certain change to the flesh itself;
this change represents a release from the passibility and decay which
necessarily characterize physical existence as we know it.[5] In the
third place, though this is far less generally asserted, Chrysostom
argues, as we have just seen, that it also involves certain changes
in the actual physical properties of the fleshly substance itself.

The teaching of Origen stands in strong contrast to this main
tradition. The precise nature of his beliefs about the place of the body
in the resurrection is not at all easy to determine. The basic scriptural foundation for his ideas on the subject was the seed motif

[1] Chr. *Hom. in I Cor.* 41, 2 (10, 357) on I Cor. xv. 37.
[2] Chr. *Hom. in Phil.* 13, 2 (11, 278–9) on Phil. iii. 20.
[3] Chr. *Hom. in I Cor.* 41, 3 (10, 359) on I Cor. xv. 44; *Hom. in Rom.* 13, 8 (9,
518) on Rom. viii. 9.
[4] Cyr. Al. on I Cor. xv. 44 (Pusey, p. 312).
[5] Tertullian, *Adv. Marc.* 5, 10, 14–15. Cf. Didymus on I Cor. xv. 44–6 (Staab, p.
10). Ambrosiaster draws a distinction between incorruption and impassibility at this
point. Incorruption is identical with immortality and describes the condition of
everyone at the resurrection. Impassibility applies only to Christians, for the wicked
rise in order to suffer (Ambst. on I Cor. xv. 53: 271 C).

of I Cor. xv.[1] The physical body is the seed, or more precisely contains the seminal principle, which is to be transformed into a spiritual body.[2] So far his doctrine is in line with the orthodox view, for even Tertullian as we have seen had emphasized that the flesh after its resurrection must undergo change and transformation before its entry into the kingdom of heaven.[3] Some of Origen's later admirers went indeed so far as to insist that his doctrine was in perfect accord with normal orthodoxy and that he had taught the resurrection of the flesh.[4] But in this they were almost certainly claiming too much. The outline form of Origen's doctrine is the same as that of the more literal orthodoxy because both built upon Paul's concept of the seed, but the detailed filling out of that form is different. The body is to enter into heaven, clothed upon and transformed by God. For the orthodox such transformation was normally understood to involve a change in the body's desires rather than in its physical structure.[5] Thus Methodius argues that Paul uses not only the analogy of the seed but also that of sleep, where the significance must be found in the continuity between the two rather than the change.[6] Origen also is insistent that the resurrection of the Christian is a bodily one and no purely allegorical concept. He even uses the traditional argument that Paul's words about being sown in corruption are inapplicable to the soul and must refer to the body alone.[7] The Christian's resurrection derives from the resurrection of Christ, the first-fruit of those who have slept, and it must therefore be of the same fundamental character.[8] But Christ's body

---

[1] De Principiis, 2, 10, 1–3; 3, 6, 4–7; Con. Cel. 5, 18–19.

[2] Con. Cel. 5, 23; 7, 38. Cf. H. Chadwick, 'Origen, Celsus and the Stoa', H.T.R. XLI (1948), 101.   [3] Cf. p. 46 above.

[4] E.g. Pamphilus, Apologia pro Origene, 7 (P.G. 17, 594–601). This was one of the main issues on which Origen was regarded as suspect at the time of Rufinus' translations, and we have therefore to be especially cautious in using passages on this subject which have come down to us only in the form of Latin translations.

[5] Methodius, De Res. 3, 16, 5. In the light of the teaching of Chrysostom (see p. 46 above) this must be regarded as an approximate rather than a precise distinction between orthodox teaching and that of Origen.   [6] Ibid. 1, 53, 3.

[7] Pamphilus, Apologia, 7 (P.G. 17, 598 B), quoting from Origen's 28th Homily on Isaiah.

[8] Origen, Frags. on I Cor. xv. 12 and I Cor. xv. 20 (J.T.S. x, 44–5, 45–6). Cf. Pamphilus, Apologia, 7 (P.G. 17, 600 A), quoting from Origen's Commentary on Ps. xv (xvi). 9.

was certainly not of a straightforward fleshly character; he may have eaten and drunk after his resurrection and allowed himself to be touched in order to convince the doubting apostles, but his ability to pass through closed doors and to disappear at will is a better indication of the real nature of his body as etherial and spiritual.[1] For Origen indeed the transformation of the body appears to have involved the eventual elimination of the flesh altogether.[2] Origen's objections to the idea of the resurrection of the flesh were based on current philosophical notions rather than on directly biblical grounds,[3] but it is clear from what we have already seen that he felt such views to be fully consistent with his general exegesis of Paul's teaching. The exact nature of Origen's positive assertions about the spiritual body is the point which is most difficult to determine. It is clear that the later charge that he taught that the disembodied soul would be spherical in shape is unfounded.[4] He seems rather to have insisted that, though the body would be no longer a body of flesh, it would be continuous with the old body in form. Thus the element of continuity, which for the majority of orthodox writers was a most important part of the significance of the restoration of the flesh, seems for Origen to have been expressed by the idea of the continuation of the same form.[5]

[1] Jerome, *Con. Joh. Hier.* 26 (*P.L.* 23, 378 A–379 A).
[2] J. Daniélou, *Origène* (1948), pp. 215–16 (E.T. p. 218).
[3] H. Chadwick, 'Origen, Celsus and the Stoa', pp. 86–94.
[4] *Ibid.* pp. 95–102.
[5] *Ibid.* p. 99; H. Crouzel, *Théologie*, p. 249. See Origen, *Sel. in Ps.* i. 5 (*P.G.* 12, 1093 B, C); Methodius, *De Res.* 1, 22, 3–5; Jerome, *Con. Joh. Hier.* 25–6 (*P.L.* 23, 376 C).

CHAPTER IV

THE LAW

We have little precise knowledge of Marcion's own exegesis, but his influence upon the exegesis of orthodox Christian writers is evident at every point. He is like a figure standing just off-stage but casting his shadow over every player on it. Paul's own attitude to the law was ambivalent to a degree which has seemed to not a few to involve him in inconsistency and contradiction.[1] Marcion's radical separation of law and gospel, which Tertullian describes as 'his special and principal work', was derived primarily from the writings of Paul.[2] The new creation of II Cor. v. 17 was evidence to him of the fundamental newness of the gospel,[3] while he interpreted such texts as Rom. iii. 20, Gal. iii. 13 and Col. ii. 18 as showing an unqualified disparagement of the law.[4] This attack upon the law was a matter of vital concern to every orthodox Christian. It struck at the roots of the fundamental Christian conviction that the revelation of God in Christ was in direct continuity with the revelation of the same God in the era of the Old Testament. It had therefore to be controverted by all possible means. Every opportunity was taken to deny the existence of any such division between law and gospel in Paul's teaching. Cyril of Jerusalem, for example, declares that Paul remained a persecutor of the Church as long as he believed that Christianity abrogated the law rather than fulfilled it, and Pelagius even asserts that the fact that there are ten Pauline letters (including Hebrews but excluding those addressed to individuals) was deliberately intended by Paul himself to signify his fundamental agreement

---

[1] E.g. W. D. Davies, *Paul and Rabbinic Judaism* (1955), p. 71, where he speaks of 'Paul's contradictory attitudes to the Torah'; M. Simon, *Verus Israel* (1948), p. 98.

[2] *Adv. Marc.* 1, 19, 4.

[3] Adamantius, *Dialogos*, 2, 16. Orthodox commentators did not need to deny that old and new here referred to law and grace; they found their answer to Marcion in the opening words of *v.* 18, 'All are from God' (Severian, *in loc.*—Staab, p. 293; Didymus, *in loc.*—Staab, p. 29).

[4] Origen, *Comm. in Rom.* 3, 6 (941 A); Jerome on Gal. iii. 13 (360 A); Tertullian, *Adv. Marc.* 5, 19, 9–11. For some further examples of Paul's language used to disparage the law, see Hegemonius, *Acta Archelai*, 45.

with the ten laws of Moses.[1] But more was needed than mere assertions of this kind. It was through his interpretation of Paul's
epistles that Marcion had been able to ground his ideas in Christian
Scripture; it was at that point therefore that it was particularly
important to show him to have been wrong. This objective in
Pauline exegesis was most strongly felt in the years closest to Marcion's own lifetime, but its influence continued largely unabated
throughout the patristic period. Where Marcion's emphasis had
fallen with extreme one-sidedness on Paul's criticisms of the law,
the emphasis of the orthodox commentators falls almost equally
heavily on the other side, on the positive aspects of Paul's attitude.
In the more detailed task of the interpretation of Paul's teaching
about the law many varied lines of reasoning are to be found in
their work, but all of them serve in one way or another to ensure that
the element of Paul's opposition to the law is kept to a minimum.

I. DIFFERENT SENSES OF THE WORD 'LAW'

First of all it has to be remembered that not every occurrence of the
word 'law' in Paul's writings necessarily refers to the Mosaic law
of the Old Testament. In the Epistle to the Romans he clearly
speaks of natural law in ch. ii, of the law of my mind and an opposing
law in my members in ch. vii and of the law of sin and death and
the law of the spirit of life in ch. viii. It is therefore always possible
for the commentator to claim that apparently derogatory remarks
about the 'law' do not refer to the law of Moses at all, but are examples
of some other sense of the word 'law'. Thus Tertullian asserts that the
law which is 'the power of sin' is to be understood as the 'law
which is in my members warring against the law of my mind'.[2]

It is in Origen's commentary on Romans that this principle of
interpretation finds its most thoroughgoing application. Origen
insists that the word 'law' is used by Paul in a variety of senses and
that a careful distinction between these senses is essential if we are
not to misunderstand his meaning.[3] He lists six different senses in

[1] Cyril, *Catecheses*, 10, 18; Pelagius, p. 3.
[2] *De Res. Mort.* 51, 6 (I Cor. xv. 56: Rom. vii. 23).
[3] Origen on Rom. iii. 19 (Scherer, p. 144; *Comm. in Rom.* 3, 6—937 C); Frag. on
Rom. iv. 15–17 (*J.T.S.* XIII, 359; *Comm. in Rom.* 4, 4—972 B).

which the word is used and illustrates them all from Paul's writing:
(i) the Mosaic law according to the letter (Gal. iii. 10, 19, 24; v. 4);
(ii) the Mosaic law according to its spiritual sense (Rom. vii. 12, 14);
(iii) natural law (Rom. ii. 14); (iv) the Mosaic history (Gal. iv. 2);
(v) the prophetic books (I Cor. xiv. 21); (vi)—though this last
sense is added somewhat tentatively—the teachings of Christ
(I Cor. ix. 21).[1] He suggests that the presence or absence of the
article can help us to distinguish between the references to the law
of Moses and to natural law, but he never claims that this is an
invariable rule.[2] In ch. iv, for example, where law is contrasted with
promise as the basis of God's dealings with Abraham, he prefers in
the light of the context to take the passage as referring to the law of
Moses in spite of the absence of the article; he does, however,
claim that the passage could be taken to refer to natural law, which in
its turn is clearly to be distinguished from the law of faith.[3] Natural
law is in fact the most frequent of all the different uses in the epistle.[4]
Romans iii. 19, which speaks of the law reducing every mouth to
silence before God, must be a reference to the natural rather than the
Mosaic law, because only so could the universal nature of the
conclusion be justified.[5] Passages which speak of the law making
men responsible for their sin are normally interpreted as referring
to natural law; the period of man's innocence is to be understood
less as a pre-Mosaic historical period than as that of children below the age of moral awareness.[6] Such an interpretation is very
difficult to carry through with consistency in Rom. v, where a period

---

[1] Origen, Frag. on Rom. ii. 21–5 (*J.T.S.* xiii, 216); on Rom. vii. 7 (*J.T.S.* xiv, 11–12). On the whole subject see R. Hanson, *Allegory and Event* (1959), pp. 298–300. On the last point—an interpretation of νόμος in I Cor. ix. 21 as implying the teachings of Christ—cf. C. H. Dodd, 'ΕΝΝΟΜΟΣ ΧΡΙΣΤΟΥ', in *Studia Paulina in honorem J. de Zwaan* (1953), pp. 96–110.

[2] Origen, *Comm. in Rom.* 3, 7 (944A, B) on Rom. iii. 21.

[3] *Ibid.* 4, 3 (970C, D) on Rom. iv. 13.

[4] *Ibid.* 5, 1 (1014A) on Rom. v. 13.

[5] Origen on Rom. iii. 19 (Scherer, p. 144; *J.T.S.* xiii, 220; *Comm. in Rom.* 3, 6—937D–938C). Ambrosiaster opposes this argument on the ground that in the context the sin of the Greek world is taken for granted (Ambst. *in loc.*—78A, B).

[6] Origen on Rom. iii. 9–18 (Scherer, p. 136; *Comm. in Rom.* 3, 2—930C, D); on Rom. iii. 19 (Scherer, pp. 144–6; *J.T.S.* xiii, 220; *Comm. in Rom.* 3, 6—938B,C); *Comm. in Rom.* 5, 1 (1014A) on Rom. v. 13; Frag. on Rom. vii. 7–11 (*J.T.S.* xiv, 14; *Comm. in Rom.* 6, 8—1082A); *Comm. in Joann.* 2, 15.

from Adam to Moses is explicitly mentioned. In arguing with Celsus, Origen insists that Adam means 'man' and what is said about him is meant to be interpreted philosophically as referring to the whole race rather than to a particular individual.[1] But in the detailed work of exegesis it is not so easy to dismiss the historical aspect of the passage as a whole.[2] In his commentary therefore, while not omitting altogether the kind of idea represented in the *Contra Celsum*, his main line of reasoning is an altogether different one, based rather upon the significance of the name Moses than upon that of the name Adam. In this passage, he argues, Moses is to be identified with 'law' and can be referred to the whole reign of law up to its end and not simply to its beginning; the period from Adam to Moses means therefore in fact the whole period from Adam to Christ.[3] In so far as the introduction of the law of Moses does represent a new stage in God's dealing with the problem of man's sin, it must be understood as the preliminary stages of man's cure.[4] On no account may any increase of sin be attributed to the coming of the Mosaic law; that would be to fall into the heresy of Marcion. Thus Rom. v. 20 must be understood as referring either to natural law or better still to the law in my members.[5]

There is nothing, Origen declares, to be surprised at in all this. It is a common scriptural practice for words to be used with more than one meaning, and if this is once recognized as a basic principle of exegesis in the interpretation of this whole subject, the element of apparent contradiction in Paul's teaching about the law is effectively removed.[6] This can hardly be denied, though it may be claimed in reply that the contradiction requires to be explained rather than removed. Certainly its removal by these means can only be carried out, as Origen himself is forced to admit, at a considerable cost;

---

[1] *Con. Cel.* 4, 40.

[2] Cf., for example, the argument of Acacius of Caesarea, who says that Adam must be understood historically in this passage and not as a purely typical figure on the ground that only so can any sense be given to the concept of 'those who have sinned not in the likeness of Adam's transgression' (on Rom. v. 14—Staab, p. 53).

[3] Origen, *Comm. in Rom.* 5, 1 (1018 A) on Rom. v. 14; *Comm. in Joann.* 20, 39. Cf. Augustine, *Expos. Prop. Ep. ad Rom.* 29 (Rom. v. 14).

[4] Origen, *Comm. in Rom.* 5, 1 (1017 C) on Rom. v. 14.

[5] *Ibid.* 5, 6 (1033 A, B).

[6] Origen on Rom. iii. 21 (Scherer, pp. 150–2; *Comm. in Rom.* 3, 7—942 B).

when the principle is applied to the discussion of law in Rom. vii, Origen is involved in saying that the senses of the word 'law' change with great frequency and without any explicit indications of the changes. He himself, as we have seen, is unperturbed by the necessity of making such an admission and even in this extreme form had no difficulty in integrating it into his general beliefs about the form of scripture.[1] But it is hardly surprising that a theory requiring so unusual a justification was not maintained in this developed form by subsequent commentators. Thus Chrysostom, whose emphasis lies always on the continuity of the argument in a biblical passage and on the clarity of its revelation, will have nothing to do with it. He is perfectly capable of recognizing the existence of different senses of the word 'law' in Paul's writings. Thus in Rom. ii. 14–15 he distinguishes within the two verses the three senses of written law, natural law and law revealed in action.[2] Elsewhere he points out that Paul sometimes uses the word to mean the whole Old Testament.[3] But when he comes to the central section of Rom. vii he is quite clear that the context requires an interpretation in terms of the Mosaic law throughout and that the various other suggested lines of interpretation in terms of natural law or the paradisal command must be ruled out altogether.[4]

The position with regard to the closing verses of Rom. vii is rather different. There Paul does use the word 'law' in a variety of senses, but he is quite explicit about the fact that he is doing so. Various writers attempt to systematize these fluctuating senses. Thus Methodius suggests either a fourfold scheme consisting of two opposing pairs—the law of God over against the law of the devil and the law of my mind over against the law of sin—or alternatively a threefold scheme—God's written law, the law of my mind and the law of sin.[5] But Theodore insists that commentators who puzzle over the relative merits of a three- or fourfold analysis are creating unnecessary difficulties for themselves; Paul does not jump arbitrarily

[1] See p. 17 above.
[2] Chr. *Hom. in Rom.* 6, 2 (9, 435) on Rom. ii. 25.
[3] *Ibid.* 7, 1 (9, 441) on Rom. iii. 19.
[4] *Ibid.* 12, 6 (9, 502) on Rom. vii. 12.
[5] Methodius on Rom. vii. 22–3 (Cramer, pp. 204–5); *De Res.* 2, 7, 1. Ambrosiaster gives a similar but not identical fourfold analysis (Ambst. on Rom. vii. 23—114A, B).

from one sense of the word 'law' to another; if he wishes to introduce a new sense of the word, he explicitly defines it by some qualifying word or phrase—as 'law of sin' or 'law of the spirit of life'—and the exegete is left in no doubt as to his meaning.[1]

In this kind of way the volume of Paul's apparent invective against the Mosaic law was patient of a considerable measure of reduction. Nevertheless, not even Origen, who used it most extensively, could claim that it provided a total answer to the problem. There were still undoubted references to the Mosaic law which were felt to require careful exegesis if Paul's writings were to be kept free from a radically Marcionite interpretation.

2. THE RELATION OF LAW AND SIN

A second characteristic of all exegetical work on this subject is a careful insistence that the close association between the law and sin which is so prominent a feature of Paul's thought is of a kind which does not imply any derogation of the law itself. Origen, as we have seen, is reluctant to admit any connection between the law of Moses and sin other than a prohibitive and preventive one, though even he is forced on occasions to allow the existence of connections other than these obviously beneficial ones. No other writer shows the same degree of reluctance as Origen in this matter; but, however far they go in admitting even a causal relationship between the law and sin, all are careful to defend the law itself from ultimate blame.

The basic position of all the interpreters is a recognition of the position of the law as a kind of half-way stage between the sin of Adam and the redeeming work of Christ. Cyril of Alexandria, for example, finds this idea implicit in the use of the word παρεισῆλθεν ('came in beside') in Rom. v. 20.[2] The idea reaches its full development in Augustine's careful delineation of four stages—before law, when the downward pull of sin goes altogether unchecked; under law, when man can will not to want to sin but cannot avoid sinning; grace, when he receives the power to overcome the lure of sin; peace, when in the life to come the pull of sin is removed

---

[1] Theod. on Rom. vii. 22–3 (Staab, pp. 132–3).
[2] Cyr. Al. *in loc.* (Pusey, p. 187).

altogether.[1] But quite apart from and long before any such schematic working out of the idea, it was clearly grasped that the law had a function in direct relation to the problem of man's sin but that it was not the decisive factor in the matter. This function was conceived primarily as making clearer the sinfulness of sin and thereby increasing both man's knowledge of sin and his responsibility for it.

Irenaeus with his strong sense of historical development is the writer best able to combine this thought with a positive affirmation of the role of law in the plan of salvation. The law cannot destroy sin but only show up its sinfulness. Yet this does constitute a real removal of the *reign* of death in that it exposes death as not really a king but rather a robber.[2] Tertullian similarly declares that Paul's admission that the law brings sin to light is no impeachment of the law but rather a high encomium of it.[3] Clement also insists that although the heretics do use Paul's teaching as evidence for their attacks upon the law, they are not justified in so doing. The law is the revelation of sin, not its creation.[4] Elsewhere he describes the function of the law as 'a confining of unbelief' until the time of Christ's coming—thus using Paul's language but with a subtle shift of meaning. For Clement the phrase implies a restriction of the extent of human sin, an idea which is not present in the Pauline passages where the same word is used.[5]

The approach of later writers, however, tends to emphasize the negative aspect of Tertullian's contrast. They do not normally lay much stress on the positive value of the showing up of sin, but are more often content simply to assert that this is indeed the nature of the law's relationship to sin and that no blame is attached to it. Thus both Chrysostom and Cyril insist that the 'sinful passions which were through the law' (Rom. vii. 5) refer not to sins incited by the law but only to sins named or revealed by it.[6] Ambrosiaster indeed goes so far as to quote Paul's text as 'quae per legem *ostenduntur*'

---

[1] Augustine, *Expos. Prop. Ep. ad Rom.* 24 (Rom. iii. 19–20); *Expos. Gal.* 46 (Gal. v. 17); *De Div. Quaest.* 66, 3.

[2] Irenaeus, *Adv. Haer.* 3, 18, 7 (Harvey, II, 101) (Rom. v. 14).

[3] Tertullian, *Adv. Marc.* 5, 13, 13–14 (Rom. vii. 7).

[4] Clement, *Stromateis*, 2, 34, 4 (Rom. iii. 20); 3, 84, 1 (Rom. vii. 13); 4, 9, 6.

[5] *Ibid.* 7, 11, 2 (Rom. xi. 32; Gal. iii. 22).

[6] Chr. *Hom. in Rom.* 12, 3 (9, 498); Cyr. Al. *in loc.* (Pusey, p. 195).

and to emphasize the importance of the final word.[1] Similarly, the assertion of Rom. vii. 8 that 'apart from the law sin is dead' is not to be understood literally but comparatively of the greater responsibility of those who sin against the clearer revelation.[2] In the words of Rom. vii. 13 sin does not become sinful for the first time because of the law, but it does become 'exceeding sinful' or in other words increase in degree of sinfulness by virtue of the removal of the plea of ignorance.[3] The extent of that increase is differently assessed in the light of the various commentators' estimates of the strength and clarity of the preceding natural law. These vary from the strong positive affirmations of Diodore about its widespread nature to the insistence of Pelagius that by the time of Moses it had been almost completely obliterated from the hearts of men.[4] But whatever be thought about the extent of the law's revelation of sin, the primary emphasis is almost always that the law is never the real source of sin or death but only the indirect agent. This is the point most clearly brought out by Origen when he does admit the existence of the problem at all. Even knowledge of sin is said to arise through (διά) and not from (ἐκ or ἀπό) the law, showing that the law is only the means of recognition and no more responsible for the sin than the art of medicine for illness.[5] Where the law seems to be described as an actual spur to covetousness (and Origen reluctantly admits that the reference here may be to the Mosaic law), it is sin that is described as the operative factor 'finding occasion through the commandment'; the law is not the source of the sin and cannot be regarded as responsible.[6] In similar vein Chrysostom emphasizes that the relationship between the law and death is one of διακονία. The law is only the agent, not the real progenitor, of death.[7]

[1] Ambst. on Rom. vii. 5 (107 C, D).

[2] Chr. *Hom. in Rom.* 12, 5 (9, 501) on Rom. vii. 8; *ibid.* 13, 1 (9, 508) on Rom. vii. 15; Cyr. Al. on Rom. vii. 8 (Pusey, pp. 198–200); Isidore, *Epp.* 4, 62.

[3] Cyr. Al. *in loc.* (Pusey, p. 201).

[4] Diodore on Rom. v. 13–14, v. 20–1 and vii. 7 (Staab, pp. 83, 85, 87); Pelagius on Rom. vii. 8 (p. 57).

[5] Origen on Rom. iii. 20 (Scherer, p. 148; *Comm. in Rom.* 3, 6—941 A). Cf. Clement, *Stromateis*, 2, 34, 4; Diodore on Rom. vii. 5 (Staab, pp. 86–7).

[6] Origen, *Comm. in Rom.* 6, 8 (1083 B) on Rom. vii. 8. Cf. Tertullian, *Adv. Marc.* 5, 13, 14.

[7] Chr. *Hom. in II Cor.* 7, 1 (10, 442) on II Cor. iii. 7. Chrysostom however is not

A further argument of an entirely different kind is also used in defence of the law at this point. If the fact that the law proves a means whereby the sinfulness of sin is increased be regarded as a valid ground for criticism of the law, then it is valid not only against the Mosaic law but against law in general. But the New Testament contains many laws of its own, so that this particular charge could never be directed against the Old Testament law without involving the New Testament also.[1] More radically still the same charge would have to be levelled against the coming of Christ, for Jesus went so far as to assert that if he had not come and spoken to men they would not have had sin.[2] Indeed it would be true to say that it was the coming of Christ to the world which provoked the devil to the highest point of his sinfulness.[3]

Thus the assertion that 'through the law is the knowledge of sin' does not involve the law itself in any discredit. But as the analogy of the provoking of the devil reminds us, Paul seems to have gone beyond this and asserted also that the law actually increased the trespass. Origen, as we have seen, regarded the application of such words to the Mosaic law as sheer Marcionism. Cyril seems content to interpret them simply in terms of the greater obviousness of sin after the coming of the law.[4] Chrysostom, however, while pointing out that the ἵνα clause of Rom. v. 20 expresses the result and not the intended purpose of the giving of the law, does affirm that the law led to an actual increase of sin.[5] In this judgement both Theodore and Augustine concur with even less hesitation.[6]

entirely consistent on this point. Elsewhere he is prepared to speak more directly of the law killing (*Comm. in Gal.* 2, 7 (10, 645) on Gal. ii. 19).

[1] Chr. *Hom. in Rom.* 12, 5 (9, 500–1) on Rom. vii. 8.

[2] Origen, *Comm. in Joann.* 2, 15; Chr. *Hom. in Rom.* 12, 5 (9, 500–1) on Rom. vii. 8; *Hom. in I Cor.* 42, 2 (10, 365) on I Cor. xv. 56.

[3] Didymus on Rom. vii. 13 (Staab, p. 4). Didymus understands 'sin' in this passage to mean the devil, and sees in the idea of its becoming more sinful the fact that even the devil is not sinful κατ' οὐσίαν.

[4] Cyr. Al. on Rom. v. 20 (Pusey, p. 188).

[5] Chr. *Hom. in Rom.* 10, 3 (9, 478).

[6] Theod. on Rom. vii. 5 and vii. 8 (Staab, pp. 125, 127); Augustine, *Expos. Prop. Ep. ad Rom.* 30 (Rom. v. 20); *ibid.* 37 (Rom. vii. 8, 13); *ibid.* 40 (Rom. vii. 13).

3. THE UNITY OF THE LAW AND GOSPEL

The radical opponents of the law insisted that it was so utterly different from the gospel that the two must derive from different Gods. Tatian, for example, appears to have spoken of the law as the old man and the gospel as the new originating from another God. Clement, who was closer to Gnostic thinking than the majority of orthodox writers, is prepared to accept an interpretation of the old and new men in terms of the law and the gospel, but firmly disallows any understanding of that distinction in a way which would imply origination from another God.[1] On that issue Clement does not waver. He points to the way in which Paul himself quotes from the law, and he continually affirms that it is the clear teaching of Paul that one and the same God is author alike of the law and of the gospel.[2] This basic affirmation was accepted and reiterated by all later orthodox commentators.

In the light of this underlying principle, it was necessary to interpret all references to the abrogation of the law not in an absolute manner but only with due qualification. Passages which appear to speak of the law's destruction are to be understood only of its overshadowing by the greater excellence of the gospel. Thus, for Theodore, the essence of Paul's argument in Rom. v–vii can be summed up as an exposition of the superiority of Christ to the law by comparison.[3] The same idea of the comparison of a greater and a lesser good was understood to be the burden of Paul's teaching in II Cor. iii. The law is described there as having its own glory, however much that glory may be done away 'by reason of the glory that excelleth'. The law is like the light of the lamp or of the moon as compared with the light of the sun—a real light but an immeasurably lesser one.[4] Cyril goes on to interpret the 'from glory

---

[1] Clement, *Stromateis*, 3, 82, 2. The word used is ἀνήρ not ἄνθρωπος. The primary allusion is therefore probably to Rom. vii. 2, but Clement's text has clearly also been influenced by Eph. iv. 22–4.

[2] *Ibid.* 3, 76, 1 (Rom. vii. 7); 3, 83, 4.

[3] Theod. on Rom. viii. 5–6 (Staab, p. 134). Cf. Theod. on Gal. iii. 25 (Swete, I, 55).

[4] Origen, *Comm. in Matt.* 10, 9; *Comm. in Joann.* 32, 27 (II Cor. iii. 18); Cyr. Al. on II Cor. iii. 10 (Pusey, pp. 334–5).

to glory' of *v.* 18 as meaning from the old glory of the law to the new glory of Christ.[1] The verb καταργεῖσθαι which is used of the law in II Cor. iii is used in I Cor. xiii of such essentially good things as prophecy and knowledge,[2] and also of the transition from child to man which is sometimes interpreted to refer to the transition from law to gospel.[3] Moreover, Paul is careful to use the word in the passive voice. The 'doing away' or 'making void' of the law is, as he clearly states in Rom. iii. 31, not something that he or any man does to the law; it is something that is done to the law only by the greater glory of Christ.[4]

Other apparently disparaging remarks about the law are dealt with in a similar way. Thus Jerome insists that the description of the law as 'weak and beggarly' elements is true only by comparison.[5] Theodore and Chrysostom interpret the apparently scornful remarks about the law in Phil. iii. 7–8 on the same basic principle. Chrysostom indeed works out the argument in considerable detail. The passage, he says, is one eagerly seized upon by heretics, but a more careful examination of its wording does not bear out their contentions. The law *was* gain; it is only *reckoned* loss. Moreover it is so reckoned 'for Christ' (διὰ τὸν χριστόν)—that is to say it is inherently good, but Christ is better. The use of the word ὑπερέχον carries the same implication. It implies the superiority of Christ, but by allowing a comparison of degree between him and the law it shows that they are essentially of the same kind (ὁμογενής). Finally, even if the word σκύβαλα is to be taken to refer to the law (which Chrysostom doubts, preferring to regard it as referring to the things of this world), the chaff is a part of the wheat and in fact the grain could not exist

[1] Cyr. Al. on II Cor. iii. 18 (Pusey, p. 339). Cyril does give as a secondary alternative the more normal interpretation 'from the present ἀρραβών of the Spirit to the final redemption of the body'. Ambrosiaster (*in loc.* 288 C) gives the same interpretation as Cyril. A. Plummer (*Commentary on II Corinthians*, p. 107) quotes it simply as a 'curiosity of exegesis'. While it is not likely to be right, this seems a somewhat harsh judgement in view of its suitability to the theme of the chapter as a whole.

[2] Origen on Rom. iii. 31 (Scherer, p. 176; *Comm. in Rom.* 3, 11—959 A); Didymus on II Cor. iii. 7–16 (Staab, p. 22) (I Cor. xiii. 8–10).

[3] Isidore, *Epp.* 1, 443 (I Cor. xiii. 11).

[4] Origen on Rom. iii. 31 (Scherer, pp. 174–6; *J.T.S.* XIII, 223–4).

[5] Jerome on Gal. iv. 9 (376 B, C).

without it.[1] Pelagius indeed, while understanding the word in a stronger sense as dung, still points out that dung is the remains of food once useful.[2]

The law therefore was clearly recognized as being the good creation of God; as such it must be understood to have a positive value, though one that was clearly limited in extent and of inferior worth when compared with Christ and his gospel. How then was this positive aspect of the law to be understood? We have already seen how in such early writers as Irenaeus and Clement there was an emphasis upon the function of the law as a first stage in checking and confining the reign of sin over human life.[3] Clement in particular makes much use of the Pauline conception of the law as being a tutor to bring us to Christ (παιδαγωγὸς εἰς χριστόν).[4] He sees in the phrase clear evidence alike of the law's goodness[5] and of its inferiority.[6] If we try to penetrate more deeply into the nature of Clement's understanding of the law's inferiority, it appears to have two main strands. In the first two of the three passages just quoted, and in the great majority of other cases where reference is made to the law's role as παιδαγωγός, the essence of the contrast is between the motivation of fear and the motivation of love. This is clearly linked with the original context in which Paul had spoken to the Galatians of the law as a παιδαγωγὸς εἰς χριστόν and had drawn a contrast between the bondage of a servant and the freedom of a son entered into his inheritance.[7] In the third passage the contrast is rather between the externality of the law's demand and the inwardness of the gospel. Here the main exegetical ground is not so much the teaching of Paul as the words of Jesus recorded in the Sermon on the Mount. There in vivid contrast were set out the lower external demands of the law and the fuller demands of the gospel extending even to the wishes of the heart. It is evident that Clement's

---

[1] Chr. *Hom. in Phil.* 11, 1 (11, 263–5). Cf. Theod. *in loc.* (Swete, 1, 235–6); Severian, *in loc.* (Staab, p. 314).

[2] Pelagius, *in loc.* (p. 406).   [3] See p. 55 above.

[4] Gal. iii. 24.   [5] *Stromateis*, 2, 35, 2; 2, 91, 1.

[6] *Paidagogos*, 1, 59, 1; 1, 96, 3–97, 1; *Stromateis*, 7, 86, 3. On this whole theme see especially E. Molland, *The Conception of the Gospel in Alexandrian Theology* (1938), pp. 16–30.

[7] *Paidagogos*, 1, 34, 1 (Gal. iv. 7).

mind has been strongly influenced by this form of contrast in St Matthew's gospel and that it affects his understanding of Paul's teaching. Thus he even goes so far as to describe the quotation by Paul in Rom. vii. 7 of the words 'Thou shalt not covet' as being a quotation from the gospel, incorrectly ascribed to the law, though legitimately so in view of the ultimate origination of law and gospel alike from the one God.[1] The law, therefore, is good as far as it goes, but it stands at a lower level than the gospel which succeeds it. It is, in Paul's phrase, 'holy' (ἅγιος), but, as the story of the rich young ruler suggests, even its perfect implementation is an insufficient ground for the attainment of eternal life.[2]

A similar understanding of the law's lesser role was also derived from Paul's teaching in Phil. iii. There, and in other places, Paul draws a contrast between two kinds of righteousness—the one according to the law and the other from God. Clearly the righteousness from God is the greater and the more important, but some interpreters draw the conclusion that there is also a lesser, but still real, righteousness of the law. Origen points out that this righteousness of the law promises only 'life in itself', that is to say, a limited kind of life as compared with the eternal life given by the righteousness of God.[3] The lower level of righteousness is a relative concept which may rightly be ascribed to those whose righteousness stands out in comparison with the general level of human sinfulness; the other is righteousness before God, and it is with respect to this second type that Paul is fully justified in asserting that there is none righteous before God, no not one.[4] Cyril goes further in asserting that Scripture clearly teaches that some people, such as the parents of John the Baptist and even Paul himself before his conversion, have actually achieved such a lesser righteousness.

[1] *Stromateis*, 3, 76, 1–2. The distinction in the customary English versions between 'covet' in the ten commandments and 'lust' in Matt. v. 28 is non-existent in Greek, which uses ἐπιθυμέω in both cases.

[2] *Quis Dives*, 9 (Rom. vii. 12).

[3] Origen, *Comm. in Rom.* 8, 2 (1160C–1161A) on Rom. x. 5. Cf. Jerome on Gal. iii. 12 (359).

[4] Origen on Rom. iii. 10 (Scherer, p. 138). Cf. Origen on Rom. iv. 1–8 (Scherer, pp. 178–80; *Comm. in Rom.* 4, 1—960C), where the same idea is developed in terms of justification—by works before men and by faith before God.

Nevertheless he, and all the exegetes who follow this line of interpretation, are equally clear that such a righteousness completely fails to meet man's highest aspirations.[1]

For other interpreters, however, the essence of the contrast is between a way of righteousness which cannot be perfectly fulfilled and one which can. There are not two different kinds of righteousness—a greater and a less. The righteousness of the law would be adequate if only man could achieve it. But this, as Theodore repeatedly emphasizes, is not only exceedingly difficult but to all intents and purposes impossible.[2] This emphasis was not always felt to be entirely incompatible with the other; it is stated with complete definiteness by Cyril in spite of the apparent inconsistency with the other line of thought.[3] Pelagius, on the other hand, does set them out as alternative lines of interpretation. He chooses the latter in the light of the words of Christ to the rich young ruler that if he would enter life he must keep the commandments. In so doing Pelagius draws from the story a conclusion directly opposed to that which Clement had derived from it.[4]

This understanding of the inferiority of the law in terms of faith's ability to achieve that righteousness which the law aimed at but could not actually bring about is most strongly developed by the Antiochene writers, Chrysostom and Theodore. It was they with their stronger sense of the process of historical development who had been most ready to admit that the coming of the law had even led to an increase of sin; so it was also they who were most inclined to see the superiority of the gospel in terms of its practical power in enabling men to conquer sin. For Chrysostom this is the fundamental meaning of Paul's words about faith 'confirming the law' and of other similar texts.[5] The law is spiritual because it taught the

[1] Cyr. Al. on Rom. iii. 21 (Pusey, p. 178) (Luke i. 6; Phil. iii. 6). Cf. also Diodore on Rom. x. 4–5 (Staab, p. 100); Apollinarius on Rom. ii. 13 (Staab, p. 60); Augustine, *Expos. Gal.* 21 (Gal. iii. 10–12), *De Gratia et Lib. Arb.* XII, 24.

[2] Theod. on Gal. iv. 24 (Swete, I, 77); on Phil. iii. 9 (Swete, I, 236–7); on Col. ii. 14 (Swete, I, 290); on Rom. ix. 32 and x. 2–4 (Staab, pp. 149, 151). Cf. U. Wickert, *Studien*, p. 135.

[3] Cyr. Al. on Rom. x. 5 (Pusey, p. 236). Cf. also Jerome on Gal. iii. 10 (357–8).

[4] Pelagius on Rom. x. 5 (p. 82) (Matt. xix. 17). See p. 61 above.

[5] Chr. *Hom. in Rom.* 7, 4 (9, 447) on Rom. iii. 31. Cf. Theod. on Rom. viii. 3–4 and x. 4 (Staab, pp. 134, 151); Augustine, *Expos. Prop. Ep. ad Rom.* 19 (Rom. iii. 31).

way of virtue, of life in the spirit, but it could not complete the task by actually giving the Spirit.[1] The gift of the Spirit renders the law superfluous, because it deals with the root of the evil, where the law can only deal with the fruit. But having gone thus far in apparent disparagement of the law, Chrysostom is quick to insist that what he has said is really 'a great and remarkable encomium of it'. It is such because it carries the implication that in the old dispensation the law fulfilled according to the measure of its own ability the exalted role and rank of the Spirit.[2] For Theodore also the Spirit renders the law superfluous and excludes all necessity for it; but for him it is the Spirit conceived eschatologically, the Spirit understood as the Spirit of promise and pointing forward to the resurrection life in which both mortality and sin are done away.[3] It is in this sense that he understands Paul's reference to the law as a shadow; it deals only with this present, impermanent world and has no relevance to the future resurrection life.[4]

This second line of interpretation according to which Christ and the Spirit achieved that towards which the law had pointed but which it had failed to secure clearly presents a more closely co-ordinated conception of law and gospel than the difficult notion of two distinct grades of righteousness. But it still allows a strong element of contrast between the two, and Paul's interpreters were always striving to present the two dispensations in even closer harmony. It is worthy of note that on two of the three occasions when Clement cites the famous text of Paul that Christ is the end of the law, he uses the word πλήρωμα (by assimilation from Rom. xiii. 10) and not the word τέλος of the Pauline text;[5] the one exception is in a passage in which he is speaking of Christ as the end of the law not for the Christian but for the unbelieving Jew.[6] Origen

---

[1] Chr. *Hom. in Rom.* 13, 1 (9, 507) on Rom. vii. 14; *Hom. in II Cor.* 6, 2 (10, 438) on II Cor. iii. 6.

[2] Chr. *Comm. in Gal.* 5, 6 (10, 672) on Gal. v. 18. Cf. Pelagius on Gal. v. 18 (p. 336).

[3] Theod. on Gal. i. 1, 4; iii. 3, 14, 25–6; iv. 26; vi. 18; Eph. ii. 14–16; Phil. iii. 10; Col. ii. 14 (Swete, I, 4, 7, 38, 43–4, 56, 83, 111, 150, 237, 290); on I Cor. xv. 56 (Staab, p. 196). See pp. 121–2 below.   [4] Theod. on Col. ii. 17 (Swete, I, 292).

[5] *Stromateis*, 4, 130, 3; *Quis Dives*, 9, 2 (Rom. x. 4).

[6] *Stromateis*, 2, 42, 5. Cf. F. Buri, *Clemens Alexandrinus und der paulinische Freiheitsbegriff* (1939), p. 70.

and Chrysostom both argue on the strength of the same text that the law apart from Christ is an incomplete concept and there can be no such thing as a full keeping of the law without faith in Christ.[1] Ambrosiaster indeed declares roundly that the doer of the law is identical with the believer in Christ to whom the law points, and that the righteousness of the law is identical with Christian faith.[2] It is, as we might expect, in Origen that this line of thought is developed in most detail. He points out that Rom. ii. 26–7 speaks of keeping (φυλάσσειν) the law and of fulfilling (τελεῖν) it. Keeping the law implies keeping it according to the letter; fulfilling it implies fulfilling it in its spiritual meaning, and it is this latter which is impossible apart from Christ.[3] These two senses exist side by side; they can even be spoken of as two parts into which the law of Moses has been divided.[4] The all-important sense for the Christian is the spiritual one, and this is the significance of Paul's direct assertion that the law is spiritual.[5] But this distinction did not come into existence only with the coming of Christ. The Old Testament itself, as Paul recognizes, speaks of a spiritual circumcision,[6] and it is to the literal interpretation of the law, so Origen asserts, that Ezekiel was referring when he spoke of God giving Israel judgements that were not good.[7] Moses was fully conscious of the hidden nature of the law's true meaning;[8] he was entrusted with the oracles of God, not merely with the outer words, and his breaking of the tables of stone showed his scorn for the letter of the law.[9] It is this spiritual sense of the law, which from the very beginning was its glory and its *raison d'être*, that is fulfilled in Christ. Origen indeed goes so far as to assert in one passage that, just as Christ is in his own person

---

[1] Origen, *Comm. in Rom.* 8, 2 (1161 A) on Rom. x. 4; Chr. *Hom. in Rom.* 17, 1 (9, 565) on Rom. x. 4.

[2] Ambst. on Rom. ii. 13, 26; iii. 20; ix. 27; x. 4 (67 C, 72 A, 78 B, 139 D, 143 A).

[3] Origen, *Comm. in Rom.* 2, 13 (901 D).

[4] *Ibid.* 6, 12 (1094 A) on Rom. viii. 3.

[5] Origen, *Hom. in Gen.* 6, 1; *Hom. in Jes. Nav.* 9, 8 (Rom. vii. 14). Cf. Clement, *Stromateis*, 3, 83, 4, 'The law is spiritual and is to be gnostically understood.'

[6] Origen, *Comm. in Rom.* 2, 13 (908 A, B) on Rom. ii. 26–7.

[7] Origen, *Con. Cel.* 7, 20 (Ezek. xx. 25). Cf. Jerome on Gal. ii. 19 (345 B).

[8] Origen, *Hom. in Num.* 5, 1. Cf. Didymus on II Cor. iii. 7–16 (Staab, p. 23); Cyr. Al. on II Cor. iii. 13 (Pusey, p. 336).

[9] Origen, Frag. on Rom. iii. 1–3 (*J.T.S.* XIII, 218; *Comm. in Rom.* 2, 14—917 A, B).

Word, Wisdom and Truth (αὐτόλογος καὶ αὐτοσοφία καὶ αὐτοαλή-θεια), so also he is Law in the fullness of the word's true meaning (αὐτόνομος).[1]

It is clear that what we have here is a different conception of fulfilment. Origen was not altogether without understanding of the idea of the gospel as the historical fulfilment of the law. But his main emphasis was placed on the more static and less dynamic conception of the already present but hidden spiritual meaning of the law. In commenting on Rom. vi. 14, for example, he explicitly identifies the contrast between law and grace of which the text speaks with that between the letter and spirit of the law, and in his thinking as a whole the latter type of contrast tends to swallow up the former.[2] This conception is certainly to be found in Paul's teaching. As Tertullian had pointed out, Paul explicitly proclaims a relationship between the law and Christ of shadow to substance.[3] But the proportion of the emphasis has shifted. St John declares that, in contrast to the coming of the law through Moses, grace and truth came through Jesus Christ; for Origen the relation of Christ to the law is one primarily of truth, of making intelligible, whereas for Paul it was primarily one of grace, of redemption from an alien power.[4]

This conception of the law as standing to Christ in a relation of shadow to substance, of type to reality, was fundamental to all the Alexandrian commentators. For Cyril it is the very meaning of Paul's words about 'confirming the law' and about Christ being its 'end'.[5] In this way the unity of law and gospel could be affirmed to the utmost limit. Paul's apostolic authority could be claimed for

---

[1] Origen on Rom. iii. 20 (Scherer, p. 146).

[2] Origen, *Comm. in Rom.* 6, 1 (1059 A) (II Cor. iii. 6). Cf. Severian on II Cor. iii. 6 (Staab, p. 284).

[3] Tertullian, *Adv. Marc.* 5, 19, 9 (Col. ii. 16–17). M. Harl, *Origène et la fonction révélatrice du Verbe Incarné* (1958), p. 214 n. 104, points out that Origen (unlike Tertullian) regularly quotes the first half of Col. ii. 17 ('which are a shadow of things to come') without the second half ('the body is Christ's'). Sometimes Origen regards the reality to which the shadow of the law corresponds as already fulfilled in Christ, sometimes he regards it eschatologically.

[4] Cf. E. Molland, *The Conception of the Gospel*, p. 121 n. 2 (John i. 17).

[5] Cyr. Al. on Rom. iii. 31 (Pusey, pp. 179–80) (where this interpretation stands alongside an interpretation in terms of prophetic fulfilment); *ibid.* on Rom. x. 4 (Pusey, p. 235).

that comprehensive allegorizing by means of which the full content of the gospel could be discovered hidden in the pages of law.[1] Moreover, this understanding of fulfilment was by no means restricted to Alexandria. It was of fundamental importance also in the thought of the Western commentators. Thus not only does Ambrosiaster assert, as we have seen, that the believer in Christ *is* the doer of the law, but Victorinus can declare that the law of Moses and the law of Christ are one and the same law, but differently understood—in the one case carnally, and in the other spiritually.[2] The unity of the old and the new could hardly be stressed more strongly than that.

4. MORAL AND CEREMONIAL LAWS

In these various ways the early commentators sought to bring out Paul's understanding of the superiority of the gospel over the law and of the fulfilment of the one in the other. In their normal treatment of this theme, it appears that it is the whole law without qualification of which they are speaking. Yet, as we have seen, they did not understand Paul's critique of the law to be a critique of law in general; they could not do so in the light of their understanding of the New Testament as incorporating laws in fundamentally the same sense. Origen includes Christ's moral teaching as a last, though admittedly tentative, sense of the word νόμος in the writings of Paul.[3] He even interprets Eph. ii. 15 as meaning that Christ frees us from a law of ἐντολαί (commandments) in order that we may serve a new law of δόγματα (precepts).[4] Theodore, as a result of the eschatological cast of his thought, is something of an exception to this rule, and in his comment on the same verse he emphasizes that it is from the command of law altogether that we are freed.[5]

But the idea of two senses of the law could easily, as Origen's

---

[1] Tertullian, *Adv. Marc.* 3, 5, 4 (I Cor. ix. 9–10; x. 4; Gal. iv. 22, 24; Eph. v. 31–2); Origen, *Con. Cel.* 4, 49; *Hom. in Ex.* 5, 1; *Hom. in Lev.* 7, 4 (I Cor. ix. 9–10; Eph. v. 31–2; I Cor. x. 1–4; Col. ii. 16–17). *Hom. in Lev.* 9, 2, makes a similar claim of Pauline authority for allegorizing the details of the law, but it is based entirely on the Epistle to the Hebrews.

[2] Victorinus on Gal. ii. 19 (1165 C). Cf. *ibid.* on Gal. i. 12 and vi. 13 (1151 C–1152A, 1196B). [3] Cf. p. 51 above.

[4] Origen, Frag. *in loc.* (*J.T.S.* III, 406–7). [5] Theod. *in loc.* (Swete, I, 150).

language shows, suggest a division of the law into two parts.[1] The concept of fulfilment as a relation of type to reality naturally lent itself most readily to an expression in terms of the ceremonial or ritual elements of the law. Thus when Origen expounds Rom. xii. 1 as calling for a spiritual equivalent of Old Testament requirements, it is the sacrificial laws of Leviticus that he has in mind.[2] More significantly he declares that the 'works' against which Paul so frequently inveighs are not the moral requirements of the law but the ceremonial requirements interpreted according to the flesh.[3] It is evident that he has here introduced a second principle, closely allied to and yet clearly distinct from that of the letter and the spirit, in terms of which Paul's ambivalent attitude to the law could be interpreted. It is not one, however, which he exploits at all frequently in that way. Nor does he point to any clear indication in Paul's own writing upon which the distinction is based.

Tertullian draws a similar distinction with even greater clarity and vigour. On one occasion, it is true, he does admit in an unusually unqualified manner that the purpose of Galatians is to explain the reason for the abolition of the law.[4] But more often he is careful to insist that it is the ceremonial aspect of the law only that is finished with; the moral aspect is fulfilled in the sense of being retained and even amplified. It is indeed to this moral aspect of the law that Paul is referring when he speaks of it as 'holy, just and good', and of faith 'confirming the law'.[5] Once again the distinction is not closely related to Paul's specific teaching, and it appears to be polemical purpose rather than exegetical principle that is the primary determinant of Tertullian's position. It is a significant fact that it is in his *Adversus Judaeos* that the idea is most fully developed.[6] Naturally enough his argument is there based primarily upon

---

[1] Cf. p. 64 above. [2] Origen, *Comm. in Rom.* 9, 1 (1203 C).

[3] *Ibid.* 8, 7 (1178 B, C) on Rom. xi. 6.

[4] Tertullian, *Adv. Marc.* 5, 2, 1–4. F. Barth, 'Tertullians Auffassung des Apostels Paulus und seines Verhältnisses zu den Uraposteln', *Jahrbücher für Protestantische Theologie* (1882), p. 710, rightly emphasizes the need for caution in using this text as a basis for the understanding of Tertullian's teaching on this subject.

[5] Tertullian, *De Pudicitia*, 6, 3–5 (Rom. vii. 12; iii. 31); *De Monogamia*, 7, 1; *De Oratione*, 1, 1. Cf. Irenaeus, *Adv. Haer.* 4, 16, 4 (Harvey, II, 192); *Apostolic Constitutions*, 6, 20.

[6] The importance of anti-Judaic polemic as a stimulus to this type of thought is

the Old Testament itself. Nevertheless, he is clearly drawing upon the reasoning of Paul in Romans and Galatians for the secondariness of the law in relation to faith and promise. In so doing he makes a significant alteration to Paul's argument and turns it into an argument for the secondariness of the detailed Mosaic legislation as over against the fundamental natural law. The faith of Abraham, he argues, which Paul shows to be prior to the Mosaic law, is itself inconceivable apart from the prior existence and acknowledgement of a basic natural or moral law.[1]

The importance of this distinction between the moral and ceremonial law in the whole succeeding tradition of exegesis can hardly be exaggerated. It is to be found universally. It takes its place even in the thought of such an interpreter as Theodore,[2] who is in general better able than other commentators to do justice to the radical nature of Paul's approach to the law as a whole. But it is in the Western commentators that it is most fully developed and exploited.

Victorinus and Ambrosiaster frequently interpret the 'works of the law' as referring to ceremonial acts.[3] In the thought of Pelagius the distinction plays a still more important role. He insists that if the whole law were to be understood allegorically then the foundations of morality would be seriously undermined.[4] He understands Paul's fundamental assertions about the impotence of the law for justification in Rom. iii. 20 and 28 as statements about the ceremonial law only.[5] Augustine, in one of his later writings, rejects this interpretation as alien to the argument of Romans as a whole,[6] but at an earlier date he had allowed a similar distinction in his interpretation of Galatians. There he asserts that Paul is concerned

---

further brought out by Augustine, in his work of the same name, *Adversus Judaeos*, II, 3 and VI, 8, where the question why Christians do not observe all the rites laid down in the Scriptures which they profess to revere is quoted as current Jewish polemic against Christians.

[1] Tertullian, *Adversus Judaeos*, 2, 7–9 (Rom. iv. 3; Gal. iii. 17).

[2] Theod. on Gal. ii. 15–16 (Swete, I, 30–1).

[3] Victorinus on Gal. ii. 19 and iii. 10 (1165 C, D, 1170 A); Ambst. on Rom. iii. 21, 28; ix. 31 and Eph. ii. 15 (79 A, 80 D, 141 A, 379 D).

[4] Pelagius on II Cor. iii. 6 (p. 246).

[5] Pelagius on Rom. iii. 20, 28 (pp. 32, 34).

[6] Augustine, *De Spir. et Lit.* VIII, 14.

primarily with the ceremonial law, and the moral law does not come into the picture at all until ch. v, *v*. 13.[1]

In other writings which stood closer to the fringe of Christian orthodoxy, this principle of a division of the law into two or more parts was taken a good deal further. The moral and ceremonial laws, as Tertullian's argument had been designed to show, were not two equal parts even at the time of their inception. The moral law was original and absolute; the other was secondary and only necessary because of the hardness of Jewish hearts.[2] On this basis it was not difficult for such writings as the *Didascalia* to draw a distinction between a first legislation which is in accordance with the gospel and a second from which the gospel frees us.[3] The Epistle of Ptolemaeus to Flora goes still further and offers a threefold division; in addition to the ceremonial and the moral, which are fulfilled by Christ in their two different ways, there is a third division, which involves an element of unrighteousness and which is totally abolished. In both cases the argument is developed primarily as exegesis of the attitude of Jesus especially as revealed in St Matthew's gospel, though Ptolemaeus does claim to find his three categories implicit in the writings of Paul and cites I Cor. v. 7, Rom. vii. 12 and Eph. ii. 15 as examples of the three.[4] But such solutions were entirely unacceptable in orthodox circles. A principle of division involving a ceremonial section of the law of only temporary validity was one thing; but a principle of division involving a section of the law which (in the words of the *Didascalia*) was simply a bond and a blindness or which (in the words of Ptolemaeus) included an element of unrighteousness was altogether another matter. However much the latter picture might seem to be a logical extension of ideas adumbrated in orthodox circles, particularly in the course of anti-Jewish polemic, it could not be given acceptance. By going so far it had overstepped the mark and offended against the basic principle of all—the unity of divine origin of law and gospel.[5]

---

[1] Augustine, *Expos. Gal.* 19 (Gal. iii. 1).

[2] Cf. Justin, *Dial. Tryph.* 21; Irenaeus, *Adv. Haer.* 4, 15, 1–2 (Harvey, II, 187–9).

[3] *Didascalia*, i, 6; vi, 15–18 (ed. R. H. Connolly, pp. 12–14, 216–30).

[4] Ptolemaeus, *Ep. ad Flor.* 6. Origen does approach quite close to this idea (cf. p. 15 n. 2 above).

[5] R. M. Grant, *The Letter and the Spirit* (1957), pp. 52–4, argues that Paul regarded

5. JEW AND GENTILE

One last line of explanation of the ambivalence of Paul's attitude to
the law deserves brief mention. This is the view that Paul's attitude
was different in the case of Jews and of Gentiles, and that it was
only in the case of Gentiles that Paul was absolutely opposed to its
observance. This idea, like so many others, can be traced back to the
fertile mind of Origen. He suggests, as we should expect, that the
unusually positive attitude to circumcision in Rom. ii. 25 should
be understood spiritually, but allows as an alternative suggestion
that this more positive evaluation may represent Paul's attitude as
far as Jews are concerned. Paul's professed policy of becoming to
Jews as a Jew, his circumcision of Timothy and the shaving of his
head and purification in the Temple in accordance with Jewish
practice were all evidence of such an attitude on his part.[1] It was
possible for a Tertullian to dismiss such occurrences epigrammati-
cally as the exceptions which prove the rule, but more solid explanation was needed.[2] In general Paul's attitude was explained as
accommodation to Jewish prejudice for the purpose of securing a
hearing from the Jews.[3] Chrysostom sums it up with an epigram
worthy of Tertullian himself when he declares that Paul 'circumcised in order to remove circumcision'.[4] This approach is most fully
developed in Jerome's commentary on Galatians, where it is explicitly based upon the work of Origen. The apparently stronger
opposition to circumcision in Galatians as compared with Romans

much of Deuteronomy as a secondary law of inferior authority and that he thereby
provided 'a point of departure for late gnostic and orthodox theories of inter-
polation' such as those found in the Epistle of Ptolemaeus to Flora and the *Didascalia*. The evidence which Grant gives in support of his theory that Paul held such a
view is not very convincing. Nor does it appear that Ptolemaeus or the author of the
Didascalia found their primary point of departure in any such understanding of Paul.

[1] Origen, Frag. *in loc.* (*J.T.S.* XIII, 216–18). Cf. also Origen on Rom. iii. 29–30
(Scherer, p. 170). The majority of early commentators understood Gal. ii. 3 as
implying that Titus was not circumcised. Jerome, Pelagius and Augustine follow
Irenaeus and Tertullian (for whose views cf. pp. 18–19 above) in believing that he was.

[2] Tertullian, *De Monogamia*, 14, 1; *De Pudicitia*, 17, 19.

[3] E.g. Clement, *Stromateis*, 6, 124, 1; Origen, *Comm. in Matt.* 11, 8.

[4] Chrysostom, *Hom. in Act. Ap.* 34, 3 (9, 247) on Acts xvi. 3; *Comm. in Gal.* 2, 2
(10, 636) on Gal. ii. 5; *ibid.* 5, 2–3 (10, 667) on Gal. v. 11.

is to be explained by the fact that all the Galatian Christians were Gentiles, whereas the Roman church contained a mixture of Jews and Gentiles, which necessitated a more tactful approach on Paul's part.[1] When Peter withdrew from the Gentile fellowship at Antioch in order to observe (in appearance at least) the Jewish law, his motive was to win over the Jews. Paul had no objection to such an action, which was precisely the same as his own customary practice described in I Cor. ix. 20. Paul's only anxiety was lest Peter's action, wholly legitimate in the context of his own Jewish mission, might prove an embarrassment to Paul in the prosecution of his allotted task in relation to the Gentiles. It was to safeguard the equally legitimate interests of the Gentile mission that he and Peter put on the staged quarrel, recorded in the second half of Gal. ii.[2]

It is clear that none of these writers really accepted the idea that Paul approved the continued observance of the law by Jews. Any such observance was purely a matter of outward show to facilitate an evangelistic approach to the Jews. But, as the detailed development of these ideas by Jerome made quite evident, such an interpretation could not be carried through without ascribing to the apostles a very considerable measure of insincerity and play-acting. For Augustine at least this was too much to accept, and it led, as we have already seen, to a lengthy correspondence between him and Jerome.[3] Augustine's basic position is evident from his commentary on Galatians; he argues there that Paul was not worried about the mere fact of circumcision but only about reliance on circumcision for salvation.[4] He therefore argues against Jerome that Paul's principle of action as described in I Cor. ix. 20 does not involve any element of pretence. The observation of the law was permissible for Jews who had become Christians, provided it was practised solely as a continuation of ancient national tradition and not as a means of securing salvation. And this was precisely what Paul had done even after becoming an apostle of Christ.[5] Jerome does not defend his explanation of Gal. ii absolutely. He claims to have derived it

---

[1] Jerome on Gal. v. 2 (395 A).
[2] Jerome on Gal. ii. 7–8, 11, 14 (336 C, 338 C–339 B, 342 A).
[3] Cf. p. 25 above.
[4] *Expos. Gal.* 11 on Gal. ii. 3–5; *ibid.* 41 on Gal. v. 1–3; *ibid.* 42 on Gal. v. 4–12.
[5] Jerome, *Ep.* 56, 3–6.

from Origen, and only insists that if it is to be replaced it must be replaced by some other explanation which gives a more satisfactory account of the behaviour alike of Peter and of Paul. Of one thing, however, he is quite certain. The view that they regarded the continued practice of the law as possible even for Jewish Christians is quite unthinkable.[1] He does give exegetical grounds for this strong assertion based on the apparent incompatibility of such a view with the bulk of Paul's teaching,[2] but it is clear that his main objection is the fact that it destroys the essential mark of difference between Christians and heretical Ebionites or Nazaraeans, with whom he claims that the Eastern world was still heavily populated.[3] In reply Augustine accepts Jerome's protest as far as contemporary practice is concerned. He reasserts his basic point, however, with the added qualification that it applied only to the primitive age.[4] In so doing Augustine shows a sense of historical perspective, which was too often lacking in the early commentators. It is clear from the way Jerome argues that, in trying to determine Paul's attitude to the law, he has one eye firmly fixed upon the contemporary situation over against Jews and Judaizing Christians. This fact clearly inhibited any extensive use in trying to understand Paul's attitude to the law of a line of explanation which allowed in some measure for the rightness of its continued use by those of Jewish origin.

---

[1] Jerome, *Ep.* 112, 4–17.
[2] *Ibid.* 112, 14 (Rom. x. 4; Gal. v. 2, 4, 18; iv. 4–5).
[3] *Ibid.* 112, 13.   [4] *Ibid.* 116, 17–18.

CHAPTER V

THE PERSON OF CHRIST

No subject was more central to the hearts and minds of the early Christian writers than the subject of the person of Christ. The full divinity of Christ and the relation of his divine to his human nature were the themes most ardently and most bitterly discussed. The whole range of Scripture was exhaustively studied to provide the necessary evidence for conflicting schools of thought. Even in more directly exegetical work the current Christological controversies were always at the forefront of the commentators' minds. St John's gospel with its identification of Christ as the Logos and its detailed consideration of the nature of his sonship was very much the most important book of the Bible in this connection. In Paul's epistles the idea of sonship, which so dominated later Christian theology, does not receive the same measure of examination; nevertheless, Paul does make considerable use of the concept, and there was a wealth of other material also in the epistles that was relevant to Christological thought and discussion.

In the early formative years of Christian doctrine Irenaeus and Origen each take up a particular idea from the writings of Paul and give to it a prominent place in their whole thought about the person and the work of Christ. In neither case was the approach one which was destined to play a major part in later formulations of Christian doctrine, but both approaches serve to bring out the rich and varied nature of Paul's thought on this subject.

The particular idea which Irenaeus takes up is that of Christ as second Adam. We have no work of commentary from his pen and it is therefore no matter for surprise that we do not have any detailed exegetical treatment of the Pauline passages which speak in this vein. But the basic understanding of Christ's work and person which Irenaeus develops from the concept seems to be a true interpretation of Paul's meaning. In the first place it conveys the idea that Christ has come right down to the very point of sinful human life where the work of man's disobedience needed to be put right.[1] Secondly, it shows that the purpose of his coming was to restore the original image of God which in the natural, as contrasted with the life-giving, Adam man had lost.[2] Thirdly, the generic implication of the name Adam shows the comprehensiveness of the humanity which Christ has assumed; as the second Adam he already sums up all things in himself, which he will manifestly do at the end of time.[3] It is true that Irenaeus goes on at times to press the analogy in a detailed way which seems foreign to the intention of Paul. Both Adams were 'virgin' creations;[4] Christ was born of a woman, as it was a woman who had been responsible for Satan's initial conquest of man;[5] the cross of Phil. ii. 8 is the tree corresponding to that other tree which was the occasion of man's fall.[6] But despite such illegitimate overpressing of detail Irenaeus' main idea is true to that of Paul and shows both the depth and the range of the Pauline conception.[7] The idea of Christ as the second Adam, the life-giving man from heaven, was not altogether ignored by later writers, but it was never again taken up in the same thorough and comprehensive way in which it was developed by Irenaeus. Had it been so taken up, it might have provided a useful link between the Christological schools of Antioch and Alexandria. For in them we find developed separately and, indeed, in opposition, the two fundamental aspects of the second Adam as understood by Irenaeus. The Antiochene Christ is the second Adam, the man who recapitulates in the sense of retracing the ground lost by the first Adam. The Alexandrian Christ is the second Adam who recapitulates in the sense of including comprehensively within himself the whole of humanity.[8]

---

[1] Irenaeus, *Adv. Haer.* 3, 18, 7 (Rom. v. 19); 5, 14, 2; 5, 21, 1 (I Cor. xv. 21) (Harvey, II, 101, 361, 380–1).

[2] *Ibid.* 3, 18, 1; 5, 1, 3 (I Cor. xv. 22 and 45) (Harvey, II, 95, 317).

[3] *Ibid.* 3, 18, 1; 3, 16, 6 (Eph. i. 10) (Harvey, II, 95, 87–8). Cf. *ibid.* 1, 10, 1 (Harvey, I, 91), where Eph. i. 10 is used with reference to Christ's second coming.

[4] *Ibid.* 3, 21, 10 (Harvey, II, 120).   [5] *Ibid.* 5, 21, 1 (Harvey, II, 381) (Gal. iv. 4).

[6] *Ibid.* 5, 16, 3 (Harvey, II, 368). In this instance Irenaeus may well be justified at least in recognizing the presence of the second Adam motif in the Phil. ii passage.

[7] This is in direct disagreement with the judgement of E. Aleith, *Paulus-verständnis in der alten Kirche* (1937), p. 70.

[8] Contrast, for example, the different use made of the Pauline teaching about the second Adam in Theodore, *Cat. Hom.* 5, 17 and Cyril, *Con. Nest.* 1, 1 (*P.G.* 76, 24 A, B).

The idea that particularly appealed to the mind of Origen was
that of Christ as the image of God. It is the central concept he
employs in exposition of the person of Christ in his more systematic
treatment of the topic in the *De Principiis*. It is true that the value
of the idea may well have been suggested to him by its use in earlier
Alexandrian writers as much as by its position in the Bible, and that
even within the Bible itself it is not an exclusively Pauline concept.
Nevertheless, it is to Col. i. 15, where it stands together with the
phrase 'first-born of all creation', that Origen most frequently refers
as the authority for his ideas. Unfortunately the most relevant
passage of the *De Principiis* is one that has undoubtedly known the
improving hand of Rufinus; nevertheless, the general significance
of the concept for Origen is reasonably clear. To be God's image is
something distinct from merely being in God's image.[1] God's
image is that which reveals the otherwise invisible, unknowable
God. For Origen the idea of the image sums up in a phrase the
whole Johannine teaching that he who has seen Christ has seen the
Father.[2] This is not to say that the phrase refers exclusively to Christ
incarnate. In fact rather the reverse. The revelatory work of the
Son was by no means restricted to the period of the incarnation. It
was as image of God that he granted to all rational beings some
participation in himself;[3] it was as image of God that he communi-
cated a spiritual vision of God to the prophets and patriarchs of
old;[4] and even during the time of the incarnation to see the image
of God required a spiritual vision distinct from the mere physical
vision of Jesus.[5] Indeed, Origen describes the Son as the invisible
image of the invisible God,[6] and uses the phrase quite explicitly to
refer to Christ's eternal pre-existent nature.[7] In so far as Origen
does relate the idea of the image explicitly to the human aspect of

[1] Origen, *Con. Cel.* 6, 63; 7, 66; *Comm. in Joann.* 6, 49.

[2] *De Principiis*, 1, 2, 6; *Con. Cel.* 7, 43; 8, 12; *Comm. in Joann.* 6, 4; 32, 29; *Hom.
in Gen.* 1, 13. (In each instance Col. i. 15 is cited together with John xiv. 9.)

[3] *De Principiis*, 2, 6, 3.   [4] *Comm. in Joann.* 6, 4.

[5] *Con. Cel.* 7, 43; *Hom. in Luc.* 1; *Hom. in Can. Cantic.* 3 (G.C.S. ed. Baehrens, p.
215).

[6] *De Principiis*, 1, 2, 6; 2, 6, 3; 4, 4, 1 (this last reference is to a Greek fragment
preserved by Athanasius, *De Dec. Nic.* 27); *Sel. in Ps.* cxvii (cxviii). 27 (P.G. 12,
1584D).

[7] *Con. Cel.* 4, 85; *Comm. in Joann.* 28, 18; *Comm. Matt. Ser.* 135.

Christ, he does so by means of a characteristically subtle development of his own. On the strength of Rom. viii. 29, which speaks of the image of God's son, Origen suggests that the human soul of Christ is to be understood as the image of the image of God.[1]

This understanding of Christ's person in terms of the image of God implied for Origen three things. In the first place the idea of an image implies an identity of character with that of which it is the image. Thus there is a complete unity of will and character between the Father and the Son, and every attribute of the Father—his goodness, even his divinity—is imaged forth by the Son.[2] This is the most fundamental implication of the idea of Christ as image, but two other implications need also to be noted. In the second place an image is something distinct from that which it images; the Son therefore is emphatically a second being, distinct from the Father; on that score Origen had no doubts.[3] Finally, an image is always less than that of which it is the image. Therefore despite the real measure of identity, extending even to the realm of 'deity' (θεότης), the Son as image remains not only distinct from but at a lower level than the absolute and ultimate goodness and godhead of the Father.[4] Thus the total implication of Origen's thought of the Son as image of the invisible God is of a being distinct from the Father, sharing and reflecting all his attributes, even that of divinity, but none the less belonging to a lower realm than that of the Father's unqualified transcendence.[5]

---

[1] Frag. on Rom. i. 1 (*J.T.S.* XIII, 211); *Comm. in Rom.* 7, 7. The same interpretation appears in the writings of Eustathius (Spanneut, Frag. 21). Athanasius interprets the words as a reference to the Holy Spirit (*Ep. ad. Ser.* 1, 24; 4, 3); so also do Didymus (in the work printed as Basil, *Adv. Eun.* 5; *P.G.* 29, 724 C) and Severian (*in loc.*—Staab, p. 221).

[2] *Comm. in Joann.* 13, 36. Cf. *Comm. in Matt.* 15, 10; *Con. Cel.* 8, 12. *De Principiis*, 1, 2, 6 speaks of the image preserving 'the unity of nature and substance common to a father and a son', but the language clearly betrays the hand of Rufinus.

[3] *Comm. in Rom.* 7, 7 (1123 C) on Rom. viii. 29. Cf. *Con. Cel.* 8, 12.

[4] *Comm. in Matt.* 15, 10; *Comm. in Joann.* 13, 25; 13, 36. A quotation in Jerome, *Ep.* 124, 2, shows that the same idea was originally expressed in *De Principiis*, 1, 2, 6 but that it has been completely expurgated by Rufinus (cf. G. W. Butterworth, *Origen on First Principles* (1936), p. 20 n. 1; C. Bigg, *Christian Platonists*, p. 181 n. 2).

[5] For a full discussion see H. Crouzel, *Théologie*, pp. 75–83.

This image-Christology was in very general use at the outset of the fourth century, but it did not stand the strains of the Arian controversy. At the beginning of that controversy this common heritage from Origen produced a certain community of ideas between the two sides. Thus Alexander of Alexandria, whose teaching first stirred Arius into active protest, speaks of the Son as 'the exact image' (ἀπαράλλακτος εἰκών) of the Father,[1] and we find Asterius the Sophist, an early exponent of Arian ideas, using precisely the same expression. Asterius indeed does not seem to have been any more extreme than Origen in his interpretation of the phrase. He does use it to show the distinction between the Son and the Father,[2] but still more emphatically he uses it to emphasize the Son's perfect reflection of the Father's being and will and glory and power.[3] Nevertheless, it was inevitable that in the course of the controversy the dangers inherent in the subordinationist strand of Origen's understanding of the term should come to the fore. In the later stages of the controversy, for example, it was much quoted by those who wished to stop short of the fullest interpretation of the 'Homoousian' language of Nicaea. Thus in the 'Homoean' creed of the Council of Seleucia in A.D. 359 Col. i. 15 is the sole quotation from Scripture and is the fundamental basis of the creed's central affirmation about the Son in terms of likeness to the Father.[4]

The first to take up the challenge represented by this apparently subordinationist element in the understanding of the term was Marcellus of Ancyra, and he met it by the drastic expedient of denying its applicability to the preincarnate Christ at all.[5] An invisible image he declared to be a manifest absurdity,[6] and insisted that the term had reference only to the revelatory stage of Christ's incarnate life.[7] Theodore of Mopsuestia later followed a similar line

---

[1] *Ep. ad Alex.* (Theodoret, *H.E.* 1, 3—*P.G.* 82, 901 B).

[2] Asterius, Frag. 22 (Bardy, p. 350) (Marcellus, Frag. 90—*G.C.S.* ed. Klostermann, p. 204).

[3] Asterius, Frag. 21 a (Bardy, p. 349) (Marcellus, Frag. 96—*G.C.S.* ed. Klostermann, p. 205). Some writers (e.g. H. Gwatkin, *Studies of Arianism* (1900), p. 72 n. 2) regard such language from the pen of Asterius as indicative of his defection from the Arian cause, but this is quite unwarranted.   [4] Athanasius, *De Synodis*, 29.

[5] Eusebius, *Contra Marcellum*, 2, 2, 4 (Marcellus, Frag. 92).

[6] *Ibid.* 1, 4, 31; 2, 3, 23 (Marcellus, Frag. 93).

[7] *Ibid.* 2, 1, 3; 2, 3, 27 (Marcellus, Frag. 94).

of exegesis by interpreting the term only of the 'homo assumptus'.[1] But this was not the main way in which the difficulty of the Arian interpretation was met. It was open above all to the objection which Eusebius raises against Marcellus, namely that it does not seem to fit the context of the words in the epistle as a whole.[2] More often therefore the phrase was interpreted as referring to Christ's divine nature, and the absolute resemblance of the image and that which it images was stressed. Thus Chrysostom, developing another aspect of Origen's original teaching, insists that the image of the invisible God must necessarily itself be invisible in the same way, or else it would not be a true image.[3]

A similar process, though one still more acutely affected by the Arian controversy, occurred in the case of the second half of Col. i. 15, which speaks of 'the first-born of all creation'. Origen uses the phrase with great frequency as a regular way of speaking of Christ's pre-existent eternal nature.[4] In one passage he even speaks of 'the uncreated and first-born of all creation'.[5] This indeed was the standard exegesis of the text in the whole ante-Nicene period. Thus Dionysius of Rome, for example, finds it natural to appeal to this text as his primary New Testament evidence in combating the suggestion that the Son should be regarded as a work or a creature.[6] At that early stage, indeed, it appeared much less susceptible of a subordinationist interpretation than the concept of the image of God. There is perhaps one phrase in Origen which is indicative of things to come. In De Principiis, 2, 6, 1 the phrase suggests to him the idea of Christ's mediatorial role as that of 'someone standing midway between the creation and God'.[7] Nevertheless, Origen does

---

[1] Theod. on Col. i. 15 (Swete, I, 261–2).

[2] Eusebius, De Eccl. Theol. 1, 20, 71; 3, 7, 1.

[3] Chr. Hom. in Col. 3, 1 (11, 317–18).

[4] Origen, Con. Cel. 6, 47; 6, 64; Comm. in Joann. 1, 18; 19, 20; 28, 18; Comm. in Matt. 16, 8; on Rom. iii. 25–6 (Scherer, p. 160). In this last instance Rufinus paraphrases the 'τῷ μονογενεῖ καὶ πρωτοτόκῳ πάσης κτίσεως' of the original by 'deitate eius' (Comm. in Rom. 3, 8–949 D). [5] Con. Cel. 6, 17.

[6] Athanasius, De Dec. Nic. 26. For a full list of references in the ante-Nicene period see J. B. Lightfoot, Epistles of St Paul to the Colossians and to Philemon (1890), p. 146, which gives an excellent and detailed account of the patristic exegesis of this text.

[7] A very similar phrase occurs in Con. Cel. 3, 34, which provides valuable confirmation of the reliability of Rufinus at this point.

not develop this idea of a mediatorial being, whose existence lies somewhere between the absolute transcendence of the Father and the lower realm of the created world, in connection with the concept of the first-born of all creation in the way that he does when treating of Christ as the image of God. But the possible implication was there and, if scarcely developed at all by Origen, it was fully and explicitly drawn out by the upholders of Arian teaching. It had a more obvious and direct relevance to the subject-matter of the controversy than the language of the image, in that it could be understood as classifying the Son explicitly as belonging to the created realm. Here also, as in the case of the image of God, orthodox writers met the Arian challenge in two diametrically opposed ways. On the one hand were those who in effect accepted the Arian understanding of the words, but insisted that they referred only to Christ incarnate or to his human nature. This was, of course, the line taken by those whom we have seen to have adopted a similar course of reasoning in relation to the image of God. Marcellus sternly criticizes Asterius for failing to distinguish between 'only-begotten' and 'first-born of all creation', when they are in reality mutually exclusive terms.[1] Theodore of Mopsuestia similarly takes the words to refer to Christ's human nature and interprets the whole context accordingly in terms not of the original creation but of the new creation brought about by Christ's redemptive work.[2] Gregory of Nyssa supports the same case by arguing that the word 'first-born' clearly refers to the incarnate Christ in its other occurrences in the writings of Paul.[3] Others who follow a similar line of interpretation are Athanasius, Cyril of Alexandria, Pelagius and Augustine.[4] But this was not the only way in which the difficulty was met. Despite Theodore's valiant attempt to interpret the whole passage in terms of the new

---

[1] Marcellus, Frag. 3. Tertullian, *Adv. Prax.* 7, 1 is a clear illustration of the fact that no such distinction ever occurred to the ante-Nicene writers.

[2] Theod. *in loc.* (Swete, 1, 263–9).

[3] Greg. Nyss. *Adv. Eun.* 2, 8 (*P.G.* 45, 501 A, B); *ibid.* 4, 3 (*P.G.* 45, 633 B, C). The texts to which he refers are Rom. viii. 29, Col. i. 18 and Heb. i. 6. In respect of the first two his case is easily established. In the case of Heb. i. 6, which Gregory regards as Pauline, he emphasizes the word 'again' at the beginning of the text and interprets it as referring to the second coming.

[4] Athanasius, *Or. Con. Ar.* 2, 62; Cyril, *Thesaurus*, 25 (*P.G.* 75, 401–4); Pelagius, *in loc.* (p. 454); Augustine, *Expos. Prop. Ep. ad Rom.* 56 (Rom. viii. 29).

creation, the difficulty of the context was still a very real one. Others therefore continued to refer the words, as the ante-Nicene writers had done, to Christ's eternal nature, but with an emphatic assurance that no unwanted subordinationist ideas are to be found in them. The Son is 'first-born' (πρωτότοκος), not 'first-created' (πρωτό-κτιστος), and therefore the text, so far from identifying him with the realm of creation, explicitly differentiates him from it.[1]

This discussion of the exegesis of Col. i. 15 has made clear that for orthodox interpreters of the fourth and fifth centuries the primary consideration in interpreting Paul's Christological texts is a determination of whether they refer to Christ's divine or human nature. Before this stage, however, it was clearly necessary to establish three prior positions: (i) that Paul was concerned with a single Christ and not with two distinct beings, a human Jesus on the one hand and a divine Christ on the other; (ii) that he affirmed the true and full humanity of Christ; (iii) that he affirmed Christ's full divinity. On all three scores doubts were expressed in some quarters at a comparatively early stage.

The first issue is a particular concern of Irenaeus against the Gnostics, and he has little difficulty in making his point. In effect he uses a threefold argument. In the first place Paul has no hesitation in linking together in a single sentence or even in a single phrase the most emphatically divine and the most emphatically human aspects of the Saviour.[2] In the second place the frequently reiterated phrase 'Christ died' shows that, for Paul, Christ was no separate impassible being.[3] Thirdly, the very title 'Christ Jesus' brings together the two names which the heretics wished to distinguish as referring to two distinct beings.[4]

[1] Victorinus, *Adv. Ar.* 1, 24 (*P.L.* 8, 1058 B); Ambst. *in loc.* (423 C). Didymus prefers the interpretation in terms of Christ's human nature, but argues that even if taken of his divine nature it can still be given an orthodox interpretation (*De Trinitate*, III, 4—*P.G.* 39, 828–40).

[2] Irenaeus, *Adv. Haer.* 3, 16, 3 (Rom. i. 3–4; ix. 5; Gal. iv. 4–5) (Harvey, II, 84).

[3] *Ibid.* 3, 18, 3 (I Cor. xv. 3; Rom. xiv. 15; Gal. iii. 13; I Cor. viii. 11); *ibid.* 3, 16, 9 (Rom. v. 6–10; viii. 34; vi. 9) (Harvey, II, 96–7, 90–1).

[4] *Ibid.* 3, 16, 9 (Rom. v. 17; vi. 3) (Harvey, II, 90–1). Apollinarius, who was equally concerned to maintain the unity of Christ's person in the different situation of his own day, uses a similar argument emphasizing the word 'one' in the affirmation of 'one Lord Jesus Christ' in I Cor. viii. 6 (*Ep. ad Dionysium*, 2—Lietzmann, p. 257).

Many of this same group of texts could obviously be used also in defence of the full humanity of Christ against the Docetists, and Irenaeus employs Gal. iv. 4 and Rom. i. 3–4 in this connection.[1] But it is in the writings of Tertullian that this particular issue is most clearly to be seen. Two texts of Paul in particular gave the heretics a handle for claiming that Paul's conception of Christ's humanity implied only the appearance and not the full reality of a human life. The first of these was Rom. viii. 3 with its reference to the 'likeness of sinful flesh'. Tertullian argues firmly that the element of difference implied by the word likeness applies entirely to the sinfulness and not at all to the substance.[2] Diodore adds that the very same text by going on to speak of 'condemning sin in the flesh' shows by itself that Paul's words were not intended in any docetic sense.[3] Pelagius does not appear to feel any difficulty in the words at all; so far from the likeness of flesh implying any difference from the flesh of others, it simply means flesh like that of other men.[4] All those authors whom we have quoted so far in connection with the exegesis of Rom. viii. 3 are writers who are in general noted for the stress which they laid on the human aspect of Christ's life. But the same arguments are to be found also in Origen. Like Tertullian he insists that ὁμοίωμα (likeness) in Rom. viii. 3 relates not to the substance of Christ's flesh but only to his sinlessness, which Origen here links with the virgin nature of his birth.[5] He similarly criticizes those heretics who interpret ὁμοίωμα in Rom. vi. 5 to imply that he only appeared to die.[6] In the interpretation of these texts at least Origen shows himself fully opposed to docetic teaching.[7]

---

[1] Irenaeus, *Adv. Haer.* 3, 22, 1 (Harvey, II, 121).

[2] Tertullian, *Adv. Marc.* 5, 14, 1–3.

[3] Diodore, *in loc.* (Staab, p. 91).   [4] Pelagius, *in loc.* (p. 61).

[5] Origen, *Comm. in Rom.* 6, 12 (1094C–1095A). Cf. Ambst. *in loc.* (118A).

[6] Origen, *Comm. in Rom.* 5, 9 (1044A, B).

[7] It must readily be allowed, however, that the hand of Rufinus may well have strengthened the language of Origen in these passages. The question of a docetic element in Origen's thought about the person of Christ is a complex issue. (See the discussion in R. P. C. Hanson, *Allegory and Event*, pp. 272–88.) It is not a question however in which Origen's exegesis of Paul's epistles is particularly closely involved. A point at which his teaching does deviate from normal teaching about the incarnation in a manner consciously based on words of Paul is his presentation of the incarnation as a preliminary stage which the believer must in due course pass beyond. His primary biblical evidence for this view is I Cor. ii. 2 ('I determined

The second text on which the docetists relied was Phil. ii. 6–7. They pointed out that Paul does not affirm directly and absolutely the humanity of Jesus; he hedges his language about with qualifying phrases; Christ assumes the *form* of a servant, he is made in the *likeness* of men and is found *in fashion as* a man. But Tertullian points out that he goes straight on to speak of the death of the cross, which hardly fits the idea of a mere appearance. Moreover, elsewhere Paul speaks of him as the image of God. If this be treated in the same way, Christ would appear to have the substance neither of man nor of God.[1] Theodore of Mopsuestia makes the same point more neatly by pointing out that the same verses speak of him as in the form of God; the two phrases must be treated as parallel.[2] Thus Chrysostom recognizes that if one half of the verse is grist to the Marcionite mill, the other could serve the Arian cause. He argues, therefore, that in both cases 'form' (μορφή) must be understood as implying 'nature' (φύσις) and not mere 'activity' (ἐνέργεια) and that this is an unvarying scriptural practice. Moreover, the whole context of a call to humility requires the sense that Christ humbles himself from the height of his true divinity; the Arian Christ could never be a real example of humility to the same degree.[3] Elsewhere Chrysostom insists with great emphasis that the whole text must be carefully expounded—the first half with reference to Christ's fully divine nature, the second with reference to his incarnate state.[4] Once again we have been led on into the realm of a fully articulated two-nature exegesis.

Thus it was claimed that Phil. ii. 6–7, so far from showing an

not to know anything among you save Jesus Christ, and him crucified'), understood as words addressed to the Corinthians as being babes in Christ, and II Cor. v. 16 ('even though we have known Christ after the flesh, yet now we know him so no more'). (For I Cor. ii. 2 see *Comm. in Joann.* 1, 7; 2, 3; for II Cor. v. 16 see *Con. Cel.* 6, 68; *Comm. in Joann.* Frag. 71; *Comm. in Matt.* 11, 17; 15, 3; *Hom. in Jer.* 15, 6; for both texts together see *Hom. in Ex.* 12, 4.)

[1] Tertullian, *Adv. Marc.* 5, 20, 3–4 (Col. i. 15).

[2] Theod. *in loc.* (Swete, I, 217).

[3] Chr. *Hom. in Phil.* 6, 2; *ibid*, 7, 2 (11, 220–1, 230–1). This interpretation of μορφή was the standard exegesis of orthodox writers of the fourth and fifth centuries. For further references, see J. B. Lightfoot, *Epistle of St Paul to the Philippians* (1890), p. 133 n. 1. Lightfoot also gives an excellent and interesting survey of the patristic exegesis of the word ἁρπαγμός in these verses (pp. 133–7).

[4] Chr. *Hom. in I Cor.* 39, 4 (10, 338) on I Cor. xv. 28.

incomplete humanity, in fact demonstrated both Christ's full humanity and his full divinity. We must turn now therefore to our third issue—the establishment of Christ's full divinity as being something explicitly intended and taught by Paul. To modern ears this might well seem to be the most difficult of the three positions to establish, yet it seems to have been the least seriously challenged at an early date. The main challenge which Christianity had to meet in the second and third centuries was the challenge of Gnosticism. The Gnostic's view of Christ's divinity might be very imperfect, but it was not the point at which he was most obviously at variance with the orthodox Christian. For Gnostic and orthodox alike Christ was a divine being, one to be worshipped and to be looked to for salvation. The point at which the Gnostic most obviously diverged from the orthodox was his separation of the divine Christ and the human Jesus or his denial of the humanity altogether. It was at these points therefore that the challenge was most sharply felt. It was at these points also, as we have seen, that the orthodox were able to appeal to the authority of Paul with good effect.

Nevertheless, the question of Christ's divinity was also a live issue. The Jews denied the fact of it and the modalists were beginning to understand it in a way which the Church felt unable to accept. In Paul's writings it is not easy to find direct and unequivocal assertions of Christ's full divinity. Cyprian has only one Pauline text in his list of twenty testimonies for use against the Jews under the heading that 'Christ is God'.[1] That text is Rom. ix. 5, which is invariably and unhesitatingly applied to the Son rather than to the Father by all patristic writers.[2] Novatian similarly uses it as evidence of Christ's divinity, though together with a wider selection of Pauline texts.[3] Nevertheless, Rom. ix. 5 was not so extensively used in controversy in the early period as one might have anticipated in view of the fact that its application to Christ was apparently undisputed. Third-century writers were always as much afraid of modalism as they were of psilanthropism, and they may have

---

[1] Cyprian, *Testimonia*, 2, 6.

[2] For a full list of references, see Sanday and Headlam, *Commentary on Romans* (1896), p. 234.

[3] Novatian, *De Trinitate*, 13 (Rom. ix. 5; Gal. i. 1, 12), 21 (Col. i. 15), 22 (Phil. ii. 6).

regarded Rom. ix. 5 as a slightly dangerous weapon on that account. Certainly Hippolytus seems to find it something of an embarrassment to be explained away in his arguments against Noetus.[1]

The real challenge to belief in Christ's full divinity, as a challenge from within the Church based upon Scripture and needing to be met by a sounder exegesis of Scripture, comes primarily with the rise of Arianism. When Victorinus declares in general terms that there are those who say that Paul held back from calling Christ God, it is undoubtedly the Arians that he has in mind.[2] But Paul's writings do not contain, as we have just seen, very much clear and incontrovertible evidence with which such a challenge could be met. Rom. ix. 5 was of course the most obvious piece of direct evidence, and Gregory of Nyssa points out that it speaks of Christ not merely as 'God' (θεός) (which the Arians were prepared to accept but interpreted in their own way) but more fully as 'God over all' (θεὸς ἐπὶ πάντων).[3] Other texts were also put forward as direct evidence of full divinity, such as Phil. ii. 6, which we have already considered, II Cor. v. 19 and Col. ii. 9.[4] But the main line of answer on the part of orthodox writers consisted rather in finding an explanation for those texts which seemed to their opponents to point away from the fact of Christ's full divinity. The kind of difficulty which they had to meet may be set out under a threefold classification:

(1) *The argument from 'one God'.* In his arguments against the Gnostics Irenaeus had insisted with great force on the fact of there being only one God. One of the main texts of Scripture to which he appealed in support of his case was Eph. iv. 6.[5] But Eph. iv. 6 (with which may be classed also I Cor. viii. 6) speaks not only of one God but also of one Lord. In both cases (more clearly and explicitly in the case of I Cor. viii. 6) the one God is identified with the Father and the one Lord with Christ. This could easily be under-

---

[1] Hippolytus, *Con. Noet.* 2 and 6. [2] Victorinus on Gal. i. 1 (1148 A).

[3] Greg. Nyss. *Adv. Eun.* 11, 3 (*P.G.* 45, 861 D). Cf. Hilary, *De Trinitate*, 8, 37–8.

[4] For II Cor. v. 19 see Athanasius, *Or. Con. Ar.* 3, 6 and Ambst. *in loc.* (297 C, D). For Col. ii. 9 see references in Lightfoot's commentary *in loc.* (p. 180). Col. ii. 9, however, was not always interpreted in a straightforward Christological way. Theodore interprets the phrase as referring to the whole creation (*in loc.*—Swete, I, 286) and Severian as referring to the Church (*in loc.*—Staab, p. 322).

[5] Irenaeus, *Adv. Haer.* 2, 2, 6; 4, 20, 2 (Harvey, I, 256–7; II, 214).

stood to imply that Christ was excluded from the realm of godhead
in its absolute and unique sense. Chrysostom indeed directly avers
that some people have drawn that conclusion from I Cor. viii. 6. In
reply he argues that, if the text really implied that Christ was not God,
it would equally imply that the Father was not Lord, which would
be absurd. Neither the term God nor the term Lord is intended to be
used in any exclusive way of the person to whom it is here referred.[1]

(2) *References to Christ as human.* Once again our consideration
of the problem must begin with the arguments of Irenaeus against
the Gnostics. Irenaeus, as we have seen, countered the Gnostic
division of the person of the Saviour into a divine Christ and a
human Jesus by pointing to the way in which Paul linked closely
together the divine and the human, and frequently associated
the name of Christ not only with attributes of a divine but also with
those of a fully human character, such as being born or dying.[2]
But those passages which had served Irenaeus so well against any
dualistic understanding of Christ's person could also be turned to
suggest that Christ could not be fully divine. Irenaeus, in order to
make his point, had stressed the unity of such passages. A similar
emphasis continues to occur in some later writers, as for example in
Apollinarius, who emphasizes that in Rom. i. 3–4 Paul does not
speak of the flesh being born of the seed of David but rather of the
Son of God being born of the seed of David according to the flesh.[3]
But for the most part later writers found it necessary to make the
opposite emphasis; they tended to break up the unities which
Irenaeus had stressed and emphasize instead the way in which their
different parts referred to two distinct natures. Theodore of Mopsuestia, for example, objects that, by refusing to apply the words of
Rom. i. 3 to the 'homo assumptus', Apollinarius is necessarily
committed to the impossible affirmation that God was born of the
seed of David.[4] He himself in explaining Rom. ix. 5 carefully
distinguishes between the descent from Jewish stock as referring to

---

[1] Chr. *Hom. in I Cor.* 20, 3 (10, 164). The same argument is used by Ambrosiaster
(*in loc.*—227 B) and Pelagius (*in loc.*—p. 172). Cf. also Theod. on Eph. iv. 6 and
I Thess. i. 9 (Swete, I, 164–5; II, 7–8).

[2] See p. 80 above.

[3] Apollinarius, *De Unione*, 9 (Lietzmann, pp. 188–9).

[4] Theod. *Con. Apol.* 3 (Swete, II, 313).

Christ's human nature and the godhead over all as referring to his divine nature.[1] This of course is simply that same fundamental principle of a two-nature exegesis which we have already seen at work in the particular instances of Col. i. 15 and Phil. ii. 6–8. Here we need do no more than add one further example where the principle is set forward as a general feature characteristic of Paul's writing as a whole and essential to its proper understanding. Gregory of Nyssa in combating the extreme Arianism of Eunomius claims that Paul is never inconsistent with himself; he is concerned throughout with the one Christ, but the reader must distinguish in thought between those statements which refer to Christ's transcendent divine nature and those which refer to his passible humanity.[2]

(3) *Passages of a potentially adoptionist or subordinationist character.* There were further passages which cannot be classified as describing Christ in simple human terms but which were none the less a potential threat to the assertion of his full divinity. These passages were of two main types. First there were those which dealt with the fact of Christ's being received up into glory, and the most important example of such a passage is Phil. ii. 9–11. For if it were Christ in his divine nature who was highly exalted by God, then, so Origen argued, he could not have been the truly divine Word who was in the beginning with God.[3] The majority of interpreters therefore follow once more the principle of the two-nature exegesis in such contexts and insist that the exaltation must be referred to Christ's human nature.[4] The second type of passage was that which implied some form of subordination of Christ to the Father; this includes such texts as those which speak of the Father as the God of Jesus[5] or as the head of Christ[6] or which talk of Christ's

---

[1] Theod. *Cat. Hom.* 8, 10.   [2] Greg. Nyss. *Adv. Eun.* 6, 2 (*P.G.* 45, 716 A).

[3] Origen, *Comm. in Joann.* 32, 25.

[4] Theod. *in loc.* (Swete, I, 233); Chr. *Hom. in Phil.* 7, 4 (11, 233–4); Pelagius, *in loc.* (p. 398). Cf. Theod. on Eph. i. 20 (Swete, I, 138); Pelagius on Eph. i. 21 (p. 350).

[5] Theod. on Eph. i. 3 and i. 17 (Swete, I, 120–1, 135); Chr. *Hom. in Eph.* I, I (11, 11) on Eph. i. 3; Pelagius on I Cor. xv. 24 (p. 217). In addition to the word 'God', the term 'Father' also occurs in all these three texts; the latter term is stressed as being the appropriate one for expressing the relation to Christ's divine nature. In the case of Eph. i. 3, Theodore also suggests as his first preference making a break in the sense after θεός and thus not taking it with ᾿Ιησοῦ Χριστοῦ at all.

[6] Pelagius on I Cor. xi. 3 (p. 187).

obedience.[1] In all these cases the same exegetical method, whereby the apparently subordinationist saying is applied to the human nature only, is frequently employed. Nevertheless, it was not used with equal regularity by all authors. Theodore and Pelagius are its most consistent exponents, whereas the fourth-century Latin commentators, Victorinus and Ambrosiaster, although they both have a strong Christological concern, scarcely use it at all. Both of them, as we have seen, felt able to meet the Arian interpretation of Col. i. 15 without recourse to it.[2] In a similar way Ambrosiaster explains I Cor. xi. 3 simply by saying that the various ideas of headship in the verse are not exact parallels; the headship of Christ over man is not the same as that of man over woman; the context therefore does not enable us to determine the nature of God's headship of Christ, and we have no right to assume that it involves any measure of subordination.[3] In the case of Phil. ii. 9–11 he argues that the reference cannot be to Christ's humanity, because that did not receive the name of God in its fullest sense, and that the text must be understood rather to imply the recognition of Christ's full divinity in the world.[4] Chrysostom stands somewhere between the two extremes. He does, as we have seen, make considerable use of the two-nature exegesis,[5] but he does not always fall back upon it. In the case of I Cor. xi. 3 for example he follows the same line of argument as Ambrosiaster, supporting his case by a useful comparison with I Cor. iii. 22–3; just as Christ is not God's in the same sense that we are Christ's, so neither need the Father be the head of Christ in the same sense that the husband is head of the wife.[6] He recognizes that the idea of Christ's heavenly intercession might be interpreted in a subordinationist way, but simply argues that it is in fact a sign of Christ's love for us and not in any sense indicative of any inferiority to the Father.[7] The whole conception of Christ's mediatorial

---

[1] Diodore on Rom. v. 19 (Staab, p. 84).

[2] See p. 80 n. 1 above. [3] Ambst. *in loc.* (239 D).

[4] Ambst. *in loc.* (410–11). Victorinus similarly seeks to get over the difficulty by saying that what Christ receives at his exaltation is the *name* of Son, which is compatible with his having always enjoyed the *fact* of Sonship (*in loc.*—1209 C–1211 B).

[5] See p. 82, and p. 86 nn. 4 and 5 above.

[6] Chr. *Hom. in I Cor.* 26, 2 (10, 214–15).

[7] Chr. *Hom. in Rom.* 15, 3 (9, 543) on Rom. viii. 34.

function was felt to be a difficulty on this score. Christ, it had to be asserted, is fully God although he is a mediator.[1] Chrysostom is particularly concerned with the frequent use of διά in relation to the person of Christ. Christ is the one in and through whom God acts, but, Chrysostom insists, he is never described as διάκονος. Moreover, nothing of significance can be derived from the use of the word διά, for in Eph. i. 1 it is used in relation to the Father.[2] And finally in Rom. i. 7 Father and Son are shown as the common source of grace and peace and are linked not by the word διά but by the word καί.[3] In these particular instances therefore, which deal in varying ways with Christ's mediatorial work, Chrysostom prefers to use the method regularly followed by Ambrosiaster and Victorinus. He accepts the reference as being to Christ's divine nature but denies that the texts in question imply any real subordination of the Son to the Father.

One particular text of apparently subordinationist character stands out as being of especial importance and deserves to be treated separately and in more detail. The text is I Cor. xv. 28, which speaks of Christ being ultimately subjected to the Father. In the narrower field of purely Christological exegesis the Fathers' treatment of this passage does not show any unusual features; in that respect our discussion of it will serve simply to illustrate and confirm the general pattern of exegesis which we have already outlined. Its peculiar interest derives rather from the wider range of doctrinal implication which the text was understood to teach.

In the ante-Nicene period the subordinationist implications of the text are accepted as entirely natural; they appear for the most part to be accepted as something requiring neither to be pressed nor to be explained away. Thus Tertullian and Hippolytus quote the words in

[1] Chr. *Comm. in Gal.* 3, 5 (10, 655) on Gal. iii. 20; Pel. on Gal. iii. 20 (p. 322).
[2] Chr. *Hom. in Eph.* 1, 4 (11, 15) on Eph. i. 5. Cf. Theod. on Rom. i. 8 (Staab, p. 114). Chrysostom's argument from Eph. i. 1 is in direct opposition to the earlier exegesis of Origen. Origen had argued that θέλημα θεοῦ could, like λόγος θεοῦ, be hypostatized and referred to the Son; the phrase διὰ θελήματος θεοῦ therefore should not be referred to the Father but to the Son and the διά could carry its true meaning of indicating τὸ ὑπηρετικόν. (Frag. on Eph. i. 1—*J.T.S.* III, 234–5.)
[3] Chr. *Hom. in Rom.* 1, 4 (9, 400). Cf. the frequent use of Rom. i. 7 in this way by Didymus (*De Trinitate*, 1, 18; *ibid.* 1, 26; on Ps. lxxxviii (lxxxix). 7—*P.G.* 39, 356B, 384A, 1486A).

the course of their anti-Monarchian arguments as a typical expression of the distinction between the Father and the Son.[1] Origen, it is true, does know of 'heretics' who regarded the term 'subjection' as too degrading to be applied to the Son. He does not himself share their difficulty, but nor does he use this text as one upon which the subordinationist element in his own thought was based. For him the subjection of which the text speaks is a natural and wholesome way of speaking of the relation of Christ and his completed work to the Father in the last day. The essential truth that he derives from the text relates rather to the final restoration than to the precise field of Christology. The subjection of Christ to the Father is something both voluntary and wholesome; if therefore the same meaning is to be given to the word subjection in the earlier half of the same passage, then the subjection of all things to Christ must also be voluntary and wholesome, and the whole passage must be understood to teach the ultimate salvation of all.[2]

Inevitably the early years of the fourth century saw a development in the manner of the text's interpretation. There is no evidence that it was much used by Arius or the early Arians. Theodoret speaks of it as a text that was constantly on the lips of Arians and Eunomians, but it is a later and more radical Arianism of which he is speaking.[3] Arius himself was not concerned to stress a radical inferiority of the Son to the Father, and the text is not one which Athanasius seems to have found it necessary to discuss at all.[4] Rather it was Marcellus who seems first to have brought the text into the forefront of debate. To him it spoke clearly of an end of Christ's kingdom and an ultimate subordination of the Son to the Father in which the Son would cease to be Son but would be reabsorbed as immanent Logos into the unity of the divine being.[5] Thus the text was used first by Marcellus and later by the extreme Arians in such a way that its correct exegesis was a matter of grave concern to orthodox writers.

[1] Tertullian, *Adv. Prax.* 4; Hippolytus, *Con. Noet.* 6.
[2] Origen, *De Principiis*, 3, 6, 7; *Hom. in Lev.* 7, 2.
[3] Theodoret, *in loc.* (*P.G.* 82, 357 A).
[4] In this respect the history of the exegesis of this text is very similar to that of John xiv. 28 (cf. M. F. Wiles, *Spiritual Gospel*, pp. 122–3).
[5] Marcellus, Frag. 121 (*G.C.S.* ed. Klostermann, pp. 211–12); Eusebius, *De Eccl. Theol.* 3, 14, 3–15, 2.

Three main types of exegesis were followed. In the first place there were those whose exegesis stood in direct line of descent from that of Origen, even though they did not for the most part draw his universalist conclusions from it. Such writers argued that the subordination of which the text spoke was really the subordination of Christians at the completion of Christ's redemptive work. The difficulty in this exegesis was that the text speaks of a subordination not only of Christ's kingdom to the Father but also of the Son himself. But it was argued that this was perfectly legitimate in that Christians become Christ's body and Christ has so closely identified himself with us as even to be called a curse on our behalf. Moreover, its great advantage over any interpretation which referred the words more straightforwardly to the person of the Son was that it explained not merely the Son's being subject but the Son's *becoming* subject at the end of time.[1]

Nevertheless, there were others who did interpret the words more directly of the Son himself. Of these a majority refer the words to Christ's human nature.[2] This interpretation is not of course radically different from our first type in so far as it is by virtue of his human nature that a thoroughgoing identification of Christ and his people is made possible.[3] In the third place are those who refer the words of the text to Christ's divine nature while insisting that they are wholly compatible with a belief in his full divinity. Thus Chrysostom and Ambrosiaster describe the subjection of the Son as a demonstration of his complete concord with the Father even to the point of divinity, while showing at the same time that the Father is the ultimate source of all things, even of Christ's divinity itself. Thus the text is understood to affirm a final revelation of Christ's true status as God from God.[4]

[1] Eusebius, *De Eccl. Theol.* 3, 15; ps.-Athanasius, *De Inc. et Con. Ar.* 20 (*P.G.* 26, 1020–1); Greg. Naz. *Or.* 30, 5; Greg. Nyss. *Oratio in I Cor.* xv. 28 (*P.G.* 44, 1304–25, esp. 1325 C); *Adv. Eun.* 2, 14 (*P.G.* 45, 557A); Ambrose, *De Fide*, 3, 13 (*P.L.* 16, 680 C–681 B). Gregory of Nyssa is noteworthy for following Origen most fully, even in his universalist understanding of the text.

[2] Ps.-Athanasius (? Eustathius), *Sermo Maior de Fide*, 32 (*P.G.* 26, 1285 D–1288 A); Hilary, *De Trinitate*, 11, 40–1; Greg. Naz. *Or.* 29, 18; Jerome, *Adv. Pel.* 1, 18.

[3] Pelagius (*in loc.*—p. 219) distinguishes the two interpretations but does not express any preference between them. Theodoret (*loc. cit.*) gives an effective combination of the two.   [4] Chr. *Hom. in I Cor.* 39, 5 (10, 340); Ambst. *in loc.* (265 B–D).

Thus by a variety of means the orthodox commentators sought to meet the objections of those who, in Victorinus' words, claimed that Paul held back from calling Christ God. Victorinus indeed regarded it as one of the primary purposes in the writing of his commentaries to expose the falsity of all such ideas. The opening words of Galatians, he claims, draw a contrast between man and Christ which clearly attests belief in his divinity.[1] He regards as one of the principal reasons for Paul's writing of Ephesians the desire to demonstrate the fact of Christ's full divinity.[2] Once again he finds evidence in support of his case in the very first verses of the epistle. He follows up a suggestion of Origen by hypostatizing the concept of the will of God in Eph. i. 1 and developing it in a manner designed to bring out the divine status of Jesus.[3] In the second verse of the same chapter Christ is joined with God the Father in a way which implies full equality.[4] In Eph. ii. 12 to be without Christ is equivalent to being without God.[5] Similarly if Eph. v. 2 be compared with Rom. viii. 32 Christ's offering up of himself is seen to be equivalent to God's offering him up, and the unity of Father and Son is clearly revealed once more.[6]

From the examples given it can be seen that the case for the full divinity of Christ was founded to a considerable degree on the way in which equivalent functions are attributed to God and to Christ on different occasions in Paul's epistles or a single function is ascribed equally to the two together. These two lines of argument follow one another in Cyril's comments on II Cor. i. 1 and 2. Verse 1 speaks of the church of God, but elsewhere Paul clearly teaches that it is the church of Christ. Verse 2 describes grace and peace as coming alike from God the Father and our Lord Jesus Christ.[7] This kind of argument was developed in such a way as to show a complete unity in Paul's conception of Father and Son; thus Ambrosiaster argues

[1] Victorinus on Gal. i. 1 (1148 A). For earlier use of this particular argument see Novatian, *De Trinitate*, 13 (cf. p. 83 n. 3 above), and Jerome on Gal. i. 1 and i. 11–12 (312 C, D and 322 A), who doubtless derives the point from Origen.
[2] Victorinus, *Comm. in Eph.* Prolog. (1235 A).
[3] *Ibid.* on Eph. i. 1 (1236 B, C).
[4] *Ibid.* on Eph. i. 2 (1237 B).   [5] *Ibid.* on Eph. ii. 12 (1257 D).
[6] *Ibid.* on Eph. v. 2 (1283 A). Cf. Ambst. *in loc.* (394).
[7] Cyr. Al. *in loc.* (Pusey, p. 321).

that it is because they are one in 'virtus, divinitas et substantia' that Paul has no objection to placing Christ before the Father in II Thess. ii. 16.[1]

The same process of reasoning was still further extended to bring in the person of the Holy Spirit and so to present Paul's teaching as fully in accord with trinitarian orthodoxy. Direct evidence of Paul's belief in the full divinity of the Holy Spirit was still more difficult to find than in the case of the Son. Basil argues that in three Pauline passages the Spirit is given the divine title of Lord,[2] but for the most part the orthodox writers argued more indirectly from the equivalence of function ascribed to the Father, the Son and the Holy Spirit in the Pauline writings. Athanasius recognizes that this type of argument for the divinity of the Holy Spirit is essentially a continuation of the same line of argument which had been used in assertion of the divinity of the Son. In the development of the argument he draws widely from Scripture as a whole but especially from St John's gospel and the Pauline epistles. Thus he points out that Paul speaks equally of 'drinking of one Spirit' in I Cor. xii. 13 and of 'drinking of the spiritual rock that followed them and the rock was Christ' in I Cor. x. 4.[3]

The most popular passage for this purpose was the opening section of Rom. viii. The way in which the passage (especially *vv.* 2, 9 and 11) points to an equivalence of function between Christ and the Spirit had already been noted by Origen, if Rufinus is to be trusted at this point.[4] While other passages were also quoted, later commentators made especial use of this one as indicative of a practical interdependence of all three members of the Trinity, so that where one is present all are present.[5] Taking such texts as a key to the true

---

[1] Ambst. *in loc.* (458 C).

[2] Basil, *De Spir. Sanct.* 52. The three passages are II Cor. iii. 17 ('The Lord is the Spirit') and I Thess. iii. 12–13 and II Thess. iii. 5 (in both of these Paul prays that the Lord will establish the Thessalonians in the ways of God the Father and of Jesus Christ, and Basil argues that the Lord must therefore be a reference to the Holy Spirit).

[3] Athanasius, *Ep. ad Ser.* 1, 19.

[4] Origen, *Comm. in Rom.* 6, 11 (1093 A) on Rom. viii. 2; *ibid.* 6, 13 (1098 B, C, 1101 A, B) on Rom. viii. 9–11.

[5] For a full account of the use of these texts in this respect, see K. H. Schelkle, *Paulus Lehrer der Väter*, pp. 278–81.

interpretation of Paul's thought, the commentators were not slow to interpret any text in which the three divine names occurred in a fully trinitarian way.[1] At a much earlier stage Irenaeus had given a trinitarian interpretation of Eph. iv. 6 and Origen had done the same with Rom. xi. 36 even in the absence of any specific mention of the three divine names.[2] It is hardly surprising therefore if later commentators saw the carefully balanced clauses of such verses as I Cor. xii. 5–6 and II Cor. xiii. 13 as clear indications of a full trinitarian belief in the writings of Paul.[3]

[1] E.g. Ambst. on II Cor. i. 21–2 (280 C), where he uses Rom. viii. 9 as supporting evidence for his interpretation.

[2] Irenaeus, *Adv. Haer.* 5, 18, 2 (Harvey, II, 374); Origen, *Comm. in Rom.* 8, 13 (1202 A, B); *Comm. in Can. Cantic.* Prolog. (*G.C.S.* ed. Baehrens, p. 71). The detailed form of Origen's trinitarian exegesis in these passages is certainly due to Rufinus, but it is probable that the basic idea goes back to Origen himself.

[3] E.g. Chr. *Hom. in I Cor.* 29, 3 (10, 244) on I Cor. xii. 5–6; *Hom. in II Cor.* 30, 2 (10, 607–8) on II Cor. xiii. 13; Ambst. on I Cor. xii. 5–6 (246 A, B).

CHAPTER VI

GRACE AND FAITH

Those who regard the Greek tradition in theology as combining an admiration for Paul's person with a serious failure to understand his teaching point especially to the subject of divine grace and human freedom. Thus A. Puech is surprised to find an obvious affection for Paul on the part of Chrysostom, when he is such an emphatic exponent of free-will and, so Puech claims, consistently mis-interprets the predestinatory texts in Paul's writing. Puech's proposal is that there are two Pauls—*l'homme de la grâce et l'homme de la charité*—and that it is the latter whom Chrysostom really admires and follows.[1] E. Benz puts forward a very similar idea when he suggests that, while the West has accepted the Paul of the Epistle to the Romans, the East has accepted the Paul of the Corinthian Epistles.[2] Solutions of this kind with their assertion of a radical division at the very heart of Paul's thought should not be accepted without being submitted to very careful scrutiny. We need first to determine whether it be true that Chrysostom so completely mis-interprets Paul's words about predestination, whether he really fails to understand and to follow Paul as *homme de la grâce* and author of the Epistle to the Romans.

Certainly Chrysostom was conscious of a difficulty at this point. When he includes among the issues on which Paul might seem open to criticism an overemphasis upon the grace of God, he is no doubt giving voice to his own misgivings. Moreover, those misgivings were no personal idiosyncrasy, but the common view of the whole tradition of Greek theology in which he stood. The brief answer that he offers to his own difficulty reveals his underlying conviction about Paul's thought upon this matter. Paul's apparent over-emphasis, he says, is an essentially religious manner of speaking, and

[1] A. Puech, *Un réformateur de la société chrétienne au IVᵉ siècle. St Jean Chryso-stome et les mœurs de son temps*, p. 367 (quoted by A. Merzagora, 'Giovanni Crisostomo', p. 32 n. 2).

[2] 'Das Paulus-Verständnis in der morgenländischen und abendländischen Kirche', *Z.R.G.* III (1951), 291.

is expressive of a proper humility before God. But, he insists, a more careful study of his words will show that he does in fact do justice also to the human side of the divine–human relationship.[1] We can see this basic conviction worked out and applied by Chrysostom in the detail of his exegetical work.

This apparent overemphasis on the grace of God is most naturally felt in those texts which speak in terms of election or of predestination. When Paul speaks in Col. i. 27 of those to whom 'God chose to make known...the riches of His glory', this might seem to present God's will as 'arbitrary' (ἄλογος), but that was not Paul's intention; his aim was the practical religious one of ensuring that his readers will think more of their dependence on God's grace than of their own moral achievements.[2] The concept of election does not rule out the human side altogether. It is to be interpreted in terms of God's foreknowledge and of his will. The concept of God's will is included with hesitation and reluctance. It is Paul's word and therefore Chrysostom cannot escape it altogether, but he clearly feels the need of giving it a carefully guarded explanation. His normal practice is to interpret the concept in close conjunction with that of foreknowledge. The two are not identical but are organically related. God foreknows and in the light of that foreknowledge he calls and chooses. It is this fact which ensures that God's call and election are not arbitrary or irrational, not mere chance but rational and purposive activity.[3] But the element of reluctance in Chrysostom's acceptance of this idea is shown by the fact that where, as in Rom. viii. 28, the text does not specifically state that it is the divine will of which it is speaking, he is keen to interpret it as the human will and to see in it one of the balancing references to the part of man in the work of salvation.[4] Thus we can be sure that however unqualified

---

[1] Chr. De Laudibus Pauli Apostoli, 6. Cf. Origen's comment on I Cor. xv. 10: οὐχ ἡ χάρις δὲ κοπία, ἀλλ' οὕτως δὲ νοητέον· οὐκ ἐγὼ τάδε πεποίηκα ἀλλ' ἡ χάρις σὺν ἐμοί (J.T.S. x, 44).

[2] Chr. Hom. in Col. 5, 1 (11, 331).

[3] Chr. Hom. in Rom. 16, 5–6 (9, 555–7) on Rom. ix. 11, where ἡ κατ' ἐκλογὴν πρόθεσις τοῦ θεοῦ is explained as ἡ ἐκλογὴ ἡ κατὰ πρόθεσιν καὶ πρόγνωσιν γενομένη. His exposition of the passage follows closely that of Diodore (on Rom. ix. 11—Staab, p. 98). Cf. also Chr. Hom. in Eph. 2, 1 (11, 17) (Eph. i. 11).

[4] Chr. Hom. in Rom. 15, 1 (9, 541). This interpretation goes back to Origen (Comm. in Rom. 7, 8–1126A) and to Diodore (in loc.—Staab, p. 95), who also points

the words of Paul may sound, however absolutely they may ascribe the power and honour to God, Chrysostom will find some ground for asserting that the words are really to be understood comparatively rather than absolutely. When Paul says in Rom. ix. 16 that 'it is not of him that willeth nor of him that runneth, but of God' he is insisting not that 'everything' (τὸ πᾶν) but that 'the main part' (τὸ πλέον) is of God; the words themselves, and not merely an overall theological necessity, can be claimed to imply this.[1]

But if the will of God is not the sole and all-sufficient agent in the work of man's salvation, still less can it be so in the case of man's judgement. God's primary will (represented in Paul's writing by the word εὐδοκία) is for the salvation of all. It is only in a secondary sense that the punishment of the wicked can be spoken of as God's act at all.[2] Moreover, Paul carefully speaks of the wrath which man will reap for himself, thereby showing that it is something not so much imposed by God as brought upon himself by man in spite of God.[3] Similarly the use of the passive voice in speaking of the branches of the olive tree being broken off in Rom. xi. 17 is intended to show that the responsibility lies with man's free-will and not with God.[4] But Paul's language does not always contain such qualifications or signs of the obliqueness of God's acting. On occasions he appears to speak of man's judgement or even of man's rejection of God as God's direct act. Sometimes a similar passage can be found elsewhere in Paul's epistles, where the same idea is

out that foreknowledge precedes predestination in the Pauline order. Cf. also Isidore, *Epp.* 4, 51.

[1] Chr. *Hom. in Rom.* 16, 9 (9, 561) on Rom. ix. 16. This also goes back to Origen, who aptly cites I Cor. iii. 7, 'Neither is he that planteth anything, neither he that watereth, but God that giveth the increase' (*Comm. in Rom.* 7, 16—1145 A, B; *De Principiis*, 3, 1, 18; *Sel. in Ps.* iv. 6—*P.G.* 12, 1161 C).

[2] Chr. *Hom. in Eph.* 1, 2 (11, 13) on Eph. i. 5. The same point is made strongly by Apollinarius; mercy is from God but judgement is something we bring upon ourselves, as Paul teaches in Gal. vi. 6 (Apollinarius on Rom. ix. 14–21—Staab, p. 67).

[3] Chr. *Hom. in Rom.* 5, 2 (9, 425) on Rom. ii. 5. This also goes back to Origen (*Comm. in Rom.* 2, 6—883 C; *De Principiis*, 3, 1, 11). Origen finds the same notion implied by the wording of Rom. ii. 13–16 (*De Principiis*, 2, 10, 4) and Rom. vi. 23 (*J.T.S.* XIV, 368). For a fuller discussion of Origen's views on wrath, see R. Hanson, *Allegory and Event*, pp. 335–8.

[4] Chr. *Hom. in Rom.* 19, 5 (9, 590) on Rom. xi. 23.

expressed as man's choice. But even if no such evidence can be brought forward, what is apparently described as God's direct act must be interpreted in terms of his allowing it to happen.[1] So confident indeed is Chrysostom of this principle of interpretation that he prefers to treat II Cor. iv. 4 (ἐν οἷς ὁ θεὸς τοῦ αἰῶνος τούτου ἐτύφλωσε τὰ νοήματα τῶν ἀπίστων) as referring to God rather than to the devil and to take the words τοῦ αἰῶνος τούτου with τῶν ἀπίστων.

He does not admit that the more usual rendering would actually involve one either in Marcionite or in Manichaean heresy, yet he regards the apparent attribution of the work of blinding the minds of the unbelieving directly to God as more characteristic of Scripture than the apparent exaltation of the devil to the rank of God of this world.[2] Moreover, the punitive, and even this blinding, activity of God can be interpreted as beneficial in its ultimate results; it is the action of the wise father who allows his son to learn from bitter experience the folly of sin, or of the good doctor who keeps the patient with weak eyes away from any strong light lest it aggravate his complaint.[3]

This exposition of the nature of God's activity towards man has been based on the work of Chrysostom, but as the footnotes have indicated he is representative of the whole tradition of Greek theology. With only minor alterations of detail the same exposition could serve as the description of a basic element in the thought of

[1] Chr. *Hom. in Rom.* 3, 3 (9, 414) on Rom. i. 24; *ibid.* 19, 1 (9, 583–4) on Rom. xi. 8. This reasoning could be paralleled many times over in other commentators both Greek and Latin. A few of the more striking examples only need be given. Apollinarius (on Rom. xi. 8—Staab, p. 72) says that God gives a spirit of κατάνυξις only in the sense that he does not give a spirit of διάνοιξις. More strongly Theodore (on II Thess. ii. 11—Swete, II, 58) says that God's συγχώρησις is described as if it were his ἔργον. Diodore (on Rom. xi. 8, 23—Staab, pp. 103, 105) says that this is a regular scriptural usage. Similarly Pelagius (on Rom. i. 24—p. 15) describes the language there used as the regular scriptural way of saying that God does not over-rule the free-will of sinners.

[2] Chr. *Hom. in II Cor.* 8, 2 (10, 455). He is here following the tradition of the anti-Marcionite writers, Irenaeus (*Adv. Haer.* 3, 7, 1 and 4, 29, 1—Harvey, II, 25, 247) and Tertullian (*Adv. Marc.* 5, 11, 9–11). Pelagius explains the text in the same way (p. 251). Origen (*Comm. in Joann.* Frag. 92), Didymus (Staab, pp. 23–4) and Cyril of Alexandria (*in loc.*—Pusey, p. 341) adopt the more normal line of interpretation.

[3] Chr. *Hom. in Rom.* 3, 3 (9, 415) on Rom. i. 24; *Hom. in II Cor.* 8, 2 (10, 455–6) on II Cor. iv. 4.

almost any of the early Eastern theologians. In particular a number of the most distinctive points in Chrysostom's exegesis can be traced back to Origen. Origen indeed, with the aid of certain peculiar beliefs of his own which were not accepted by the main body of Christian thinkers, was able to carry through this whole line of thought with greater rigour and consistency. Origen had no need to emphasize the time element of foreknowledge in explaining the reasonableness of God's election from before man's birth. Fore-knowledge is not denied; it is present, though as a kind of logical insight and in no sense as a cause; but it is a matter not only of foreknowledge but also more simply of knowledge.[1] In the light of the doctrine of the pre-existence of human souls God need not be spoken of as foreknowing the different future qualities of Jacob and of Esau; rather he could see their souls and the differing degrees of purity which they had already achieved before birth, and his will for them would be determined accordingly.[2] The educative and medi-cinal nature of God's punitive activity is a dominant theme in Origen's whole system of thought, and the first chapter of Romans is one of his favourite illustrations of it.[3] Moreover, this purposive quality about man's apparent misfortunes is not to be conceived in purely individual terms. In the overarching providence of God (and this too Origen draws primarily from Paul's thought) one man's sin and suffering can be turned to another man's salvation.[4] Finally, Origen's universalist belief comes in to ensure that this conception is free from ultimate injustice and that no radical qualification is needed in his insistence on the educative and medicinal nature of punishment. He is conscious that this universalist belief is not ex-pressed with great clarity in Scripture. But he finds it at the end of ch. ix–xi of Romans as the necessary climax of the argument; he finds it moreover described as a 'mystery' (μυστήριον), something

---

[1] Origen, Frag. on Rom. i. 1 (*J.T.S.* xiii, 211). Rufinus drastically abbreviates this passage.

[2] *De Principiis*, 2, 9, 7 (Rom. ix. 11–12); *Comm. in Rom.* 7, 17 (1149 A, B) on Rom. ix. 21.

[3] E.g. *Con. Cel.* 5, 32; *De Oratione*, 9, 12–15 (Rom. i. 24, 26, 28). Cf. also *Con. Cel.* 4, 13 (I Cor. iii. 12–15).

[4] Origen, *Comm. in Rom.* 8, 9 (1186 A, B, 1187 B) on Rom. xi. 11–12; *ibid.* 8, 12 (1197 B, C) on Rom. xi. 25–6; *ibid.* 8, 13 (1200 A, B) on Rom. xi. 32.

not to be bandied about too freely amongst the simple lest it lead them into presumption, but something necessary to the faith of the mature as the crown of their comprehension of God's purpose.[1]

It is the claim of the Eastern fathers that a theology of this kind, which seeks to give a proper place both to the elective will of God and also to human free-will, is required by the sense of Scripture as a whole. Origen declares that those heretics who seek to deny God's gift of free-will do so on the strength of a few texts in the Epistle to the Romans and in clear opposition to the general sense of Scripture.[2] Origen is perhaps inclined to underrate the scriptural ground of his opponents' case. The few texts of Romans must surely include the whole of the ninth chapter at the very least, and it is clear that this section of the epistle was one of particular difficulty for Origen and all who thought like him. Jerome indeed regards it as a particularly obscure section of a difficult epistle and one therefore which especially requires the help of the Holy Spirit its true author for its elucidation.[3] Modern commentators are equally conscious of its difficulty. Professor Dodd in commenting upon it declares that Paul 'seems to take a false step', that 'his thought declines from its highest level' and that 'here he pushes what we might describe as an unethical determinism to its logical extreme'.[4] Clearly a solution of the difficulty along such lines was not a real option for the patristic exegete. If one is not prepared to criticize Paul on grounds of inconsistency or to accuse him of falling at times below the highest level of his own thought, then some other line of solution must be found. If the solutions proposed sometimes seem to us to be open to criticism on exegetical grounds, this is not something about which

---

[1] *Ibid.* 8, 12 (1198 A, B) on Rom. xi. 25–6. Origen derives the same conclusion even more explicitly from the wording of Rom. v. 19. That text speaks of the 'many' being made righteous. Origen argues that the 'many' really signifies 'all', but that the word 'many' has been preferred so as to leave the simpler and slacker an incentive for striving; it does not rule out the possibility of a higher wisdom being given to the more initiated. Origen supports his argument that the 'many' really means 'all' by the claim that the 'many' in the first half of the verse who were made sinners must, in the light of other Pauline teaching, be understood as meaning 'all' (*Comm. in Rom.* 5, 2–1023 A, B).

[2] Origen, *Comm. in Rom.* Praef. (833 A, B).

[3] Jerome, *Ep.* 120, 10.

[4] C. H. Dodd, *Epistle to the Romans* (1932), pp. 157–8.

we ought to be surprised. Individual points about the exegesis of the chapter have already been mentioned in the general survey of Chrysostom's position, but the chapter is one of such crucial significance for the subject that it will be valuable to draw together the main lines of interpretation given and to contrast them with those followed by the Western commentators.

The context of the chapter is the problem of the rejection of the Jews. Chrysostom, as we should expect, is careful to point this out and suggests that Paul is anxious to remove the blasphemy which would make this a ground of accusation against God.[1] But the implications of the context can also be turned the other way. Ambrosiaster suggests that Paul is consoling himself with the recognition that there is no point in his grieving over those who have not been predestined.[2] The unqualified statement of election in *vv.* 11–13 is, as we have seen, explained in terms of foreknowledge. To Theodore and Chrysostom it appeared that only two other explanations were conceivable. If election is not governed and guided by foreknowledge, then either it is unfailingly determined by man's created nature[3] or else it is an entirely arbitrary and irrational phenomenon.[4] Both these they unhesitatingly rejected. In his approach to these verses Augustine in the earlier stages of his literary career is in fundamental agreement with them. He too declares that the verses appear to endanger the concept of free-will but claims that when understood in terms of foreknowledge they do not do so. The only difference upon which he insists is that the operative factor is God's foreknowledge not of men's works but of their faith.[5] But within a very few years he had abandoned this position and was teaching the absolute priority of the divine call.[6] Later in his life he formally repudiated the position taken up in the early commentary.[7] Verses 14–19 speak not only of God's electing but also, in an apparently

---

[1] Chr. *Hom. in Rom.* 16, 2 (9, 550) on Rom. ix. 4–5.

[2] Ambst. on Rom. ix. 11–13 (134C, D).

[3] Theod. on Rom. ix. 24, xi. 7 (Staab, pp. 147–8, 154–5). Cf. Origen, Frag. on Rom. i. 1 (*J.T.S.* XIII, 210); Jerome on Gal. i. 15 (325).

[4] See p. 95 above.

[5] Augustine, *Expos. Prop. Ep. ad Rom.* 60 (Rom. ix. 11–13), written about A.D. 394.   [6] *De Div. Quaest ad Simplic.* I, 2, 5, written about A.D. 396.

[7] *Retractationes*, I, 23, 2–3; *De Praed. Sanct.* III, 7.

precise parallel, of his hardening. Origen explains this along lines with which we are already familiar. The hardening cannot be properly described as God's act; it is simply the obverse of his blessing and results from Pharaoh's own wickedness.[1] Moreover, it can even be regarded as more beneficial to Pharaoh himself than a rapid and superficial relief which would have left him without a true appraisal of God's righteousness and his own sin.[2] But when Origen is concerned not merely with the concept of hardening in general but specifically with the exegesis of the Rom. ix passage in his commentary, he brings in another entirely different line of explanation. He there attributes the whole argument not to Paul but to the imaginary objector who is clearly referred to at least in *v.* 19. This does not, as might at first be supposed, do away entirely with the necessity for the other kind of reasoning. The objector's case, if such it be, is based on two Old Testament quotations which demand an explanation of some kind.[3] This attribution of the verses to an objector was followed by many subsequent exegetes.[4] Even Ambrosiaster regards *v.* 18 as words of the objector rather than of Paul himself.[5] Augustine does not adopt this view at all; here again in the early commentary he takes a line which is not very different from that of the Eastern writers—Pharaoh disbelieved first and then his heart was hardened—but later on he considerably modifies his position.[6] He never goes to the point of denying that human wickedness precedes God's hardening. What he does later deny is that the wickedness or disbelief of such as Pharaoh 'deserved' God's hardening in a sense which is not also true of everyone.[7] The divergence of interpretation reaches its climax with the question of *v.* 20, 'Who are you, a man to answer back to God?' Theodore insists that this is not intended as a mere rebuke of man's questioning —that would be unworthy. Its implication is rather that the fact that man argues against God in such a way shows his possession of true

---

[1] Origen, *De Principiis*, 3, 1, 10–11. [2] Origen, *De Oratione*, 29, 16.

[3] Origen, *Comm. in Rom.* 7, 16 (1144 A–C).

[4] Diodore, *in loc.* (Staab, p. 98); Theod. *in loc.* (Staab, pp. 144–7); Jerome, *Ep.* 120, 10; Pelagius, *in loc.* (pp. 76–7).

[5] Ambst. on Rom. ix. 18 (138 A).

[6] Augustine, *Expos. Prop. Ep. ad Rom.* 62 (Rom. ix. 15–21).

[7] *De Grat. et Lib. Arb.* XXI, 42–3; *Retractationes*, I, 23, 4.

moral perception; it shows that the relationship of man to God is different from that of the clay to the potter, because the clay cannot argue in this way.[1] For Ambrosiaster on the other hand it is the similarity between the two that is the point. There is, it is true, a difference between the potter and God; in the case of the potter it is wholly a matter of his will, his arbitrary will; in the case of God, it is a matter of his will which is combined with justice.[2] Thus, in the last analysis, the Western interpreters reject the basic dilemma of Chrysostom that if God's election is not based on foreknowledge then it is arbitrary and irrational. God's election is based solely on his will, which is above the grasp of human reason, but that does not make it arbitrary or irrational; it is always characterized by justice, but it is to human minds a hidden and inscrutable justice.

It is from this last step that the Eastern writers held back. They were convinced that for all its difficulty Rom. ix could be interpreted in a way which did justice both to the divine and to the human aspects of our experience and that therefore in the light of the teaching of Scripture as a whole it must be so interpreted. The total biblical witness, they claimed, revealed Christian life as involving at every point the closest possible interaction between God and man. When Paul declared 'I labour also striving according to his working which worketh in me mightily', he was not on that occasion speaking out of 'humility' (μετριάζων), but setting out the true balance of the divine and the human.[3] Chrysostom, as we have seen, admits that the proper attitude of the religious man is to lay the primary stress on the divine side, and he recognizes that this is what Paul consistently does. But even if we set on one side the Origenistic conception of pre-existence as neither representative nor even by Origen much rooted in Pauline exegesis,[4] it may still be argued that this Greek

[1] Theod. on Rom. ix. 20–1 (Staab, pp. 145–7). This derives from Diodore (Staab, pp. 99–100), but in Diodore's case it occurs only as an alternative to the more normal type of interpretation. Cf. also Jerome, *Ep.* 120, 10.

[2] Ambst. on Rom. ix. 21 (138 C, D). Cf. Augustine, *De Div. Quaest. ad Simplic.* I, 2, 16.

[3] Chr. *Hom. in Col.* 5, 2 (11, 33) on Col. i. 29. Cf. Theodore's comments on I Thess. ii. 2, 'We acted faithfully in the Lord' (Swete, 11, 8).

[4] Victorinus does try to show that the pre-existence of souls is implied by the language of Eph. i. 11 (1238–42). Acacius of Caesarea strongly attacks the idea and insists that it is *fore*knowledge and *fore*ordaining of which Paul speaks

tradition in theology does in fact lay the real emphasis on the human side. The divine priority may be maintained in terms of temporal sequence by the concept of foreknowledge, but if the divine will is determined or even guided by that which it foreknows, namely the self-determined character of man, then the real logical priority seems lodged firmly with man and not with God. It is essential therefore to try and define with more precision how these early commentators thought of the nature of this divine–human interaction as they grappled with Paul's teaching about grace and faith.

Origen sets the whole concept of grace in a broad cosmic setting. In the first place our creation, and particularly our creation as rational beings, is a sheer act of divine grace.[1] More particularly he goes on to show that even if man's faith be logically prior to God's foreknowledge, yet the embodiment of God's grace in the redemptive act of Christ's incarnation and death is logically prior to man's faith. In Rom. v. 9 he takes the words 'much more' closely with 'justified by his blood' and contrasts them with the words 'justified by faith' in *v*. 1. He writes: 'Neither our faith without the blood of Christ, nor the blood of Christ without our faith justifies us; we are justified by both but much more by the blood of Christ than by our faith.'[2] The divine act of the cross and the human act of faith are both essential, but the cross of Christ is more essential. Chrysostom draws a similar picture in his comment on the same chapter. The gifts of God's grace—including first of all Christ's death for us but including much else besides—are many and various; our part— also essential but much smaller—is faith alone.[3] Theodore similarly points out that in Rom. x. 14–17 faith is the climax of a process which begins with an act of divine sending, and that this shows faith to be secondary to grace.[4] Theodore indeed, and as we should expect Pelagius, seem content with this account; God's grace is prior and

(on Rom. ix. 11–14—Staab, p. 54). The point in any case makes little difference to the main argument.

[1] Origen on Rom. iv. 1–8 (Scherer, p. 184; *J.T.S.* XIV, 357; *Comm. in Rom.* 4, 1—963 D–964 A); on Rom. iv. 16–17 (Scherer, p. 204; *Comm. in Rom.* 4, 5—974 C).

[2] Origen, *Comm. in Rom.* 4, 11 (1001 A).

[3] Chr. *Hom. in Rom.* 9, 2 (9, 468) on Rom. v. 2.

[4] Theod. *in loc.* (Staab, pp. 151–2).

is seen both in his call and in the sending of Christ. Faith and perseverance have the form of response and in that sense are secondary; but they are our own acts.[1] This distinction between the divine call and the human response is made with particular clarity by Jerome in his curious exegesis of Gal. v. 8, 'Your persuasion is not of him who called you.' Jerome says that some Latin texts omit the word 'not' but that this is altogether wrong. The point of the saying is that the calling is from God, but the 'persuasion' or obedience is man's part.[2] Chrysostom, however, is not normally content with this simple and obvious principle of division and carries the analysis further. His understanding of the relationship can conveniently be studied in his interpretation of three Pauline texts.

Colossians i. 13 speaks of how God 'delivered us out of the power of darkness and translated us into the kingdom of the Son of his love'. God has provided both the act of rescue and the kingdom to which we may be brought. The transference from the old state to the new is described by the word μετέστησε. The word, Chrysostom says, is carefully chosen. μετέθηκε would have allowed no part at all to the person being translated; μετέστησε shows it as God's act and yet one in which we have a share.[3] Romans vi. 17 reads: 'Thanks (χάρις) be to God that though you were servants of sin, ye became obedient from the heart to that form of teaching whereunto ye were delivered.' Here again the 'grace' (χάρις) of God is seen in the act of liberation and in the provision of a new way of righteousness to which a new allegiance can be given. The words 'obedient from the heart' show the place of free-will in determining our transference from the one allegiance to the other, but the words 'whereunto ye were delivered' show that even in the transference God is at work.[4] The most precise statement comes in commenting on Col. i. 21–2. In the first place there is an objective act of rescue from the power of

---

[1] Theod. on Gal. v. 8 (Swete, 1, 91); Pelagius on Phil. i. 29; ii. 13; Col. i. 10 (pp. 395, 408, 453).

[2] Jerome on Gal. v. 12 (402 A, B).

[3] Chr. *Hom. in Col.* 2, 3 (11, 313). Cf. Eusebius of Emesa on Gal. i. 4, τὸ γὰρ ἐξέληται μικροῦ βίαν σημαίνει, ἀλλ' οὐ βίαν, δύναμιν δὲ τοῦ ῥυσαμένου· οὐ γὰρ εἶπεν τοῦ ἁρπάσαντος... (Staab, p. 47). See also Theod. on Gal. i. 6, in which, he says, the word μετατίθεσθε is deliberately preferred to μετάγεσθε because in deserting the true faith the Galatians have behaved like ἄψυχοι (Swete, 1, 9).

[4] Chr. *Hom. in Rom.* 11, 4 (9, 489).

the devil. For this Christ alone was strong enough and it is his unaided work. But then the captives must be persuaded to take advantage of the rescue that has been won for them. This also Christ has done for the Christian, but it was not his unaided work. It is a joint work of Christ and man. It can even be described as the more wonderful aspect of Christ's redeeming work, because it is easier to achieve a task that lies in one's own power than one that requires the free co-operation of others.[1] Thus in the whole work of man's redemption there is an objective act of victory over the devil which is God's prior act of pure grace. But this does not exhaust the role of grace; there is also the response of faith in which divine grace and human freedom are in some mysterious way combined.

In what way then does God's grace enter into the human response of faith itself? Origen argues that faith is a gift of the Spirit and cites I Cor. xii. 9 in evidence. It is true that his primary interest in this text is to show that faith is ranked after wisdom and knowledge in the list of the Spirit's gifts,[2] but he does not ignore the further implication that faith itself is spoken of as a gift and indeed quotes Phil. i. 29 as supporting evidence.[3] But the Spirit's gifts are not arbitrary and Paul has told us some of the principles according to which they are given. One of these principles, given in Rom. xii. 6, is 'according to the proportion of faith'. Therefore by putting together what is said of the Spirit's gifts in Rom. xii and in I Cor. xii we arrive at the conclusion that faith is a gift of God given according to the proportion of our faith. There must therefore be a distinction between the two 'faiths'. There is the initial germ of faith which is something within our own power (ἡ ἐκ τοῦ ἐφ' ἡμῖν πίστις), and there is the complete faith (the 'all faith' of I Cor. xiii. 2) which can only be achieved with the addition of the God-given grace of faith.[4] This complete faith is inseparable from the gift of

---

[1] Chr. *Hom. in Col.* 4, 1 (11, 325).

[2] Origen, *Con. Cel.* 3, 46; 6, 13; *Comm. in Joann.* 13, 53; 19, 3.

[3] Origen on Rom. iv. 16 (Scherer, pp. 204–6; *J.T.S.* XIII, 359–60; *Comm. in Rom.* 4, 5—974 C–975 A); *Comm. in Joann.* 20, 32. Jerome, doubtless in dependence on Origen, interprets Eph. ii. 8, 'By grace are you saved through faith; and that not of yourselves it is the gift of God', to mean that faith itself is a gift of God (470 A).

[4] Origen, *Comm. in Rom.* 9, 3 (1212 C–1213 C) on Rom. xii. 6; *Comm. in Joann.* Frag. 11.

love from which it springs, as I Cor. xiii. 7 affirms.[1] Faith, hope and love represent a developing sequence from the initial beginnings of faith through hope to love, which itself produces a completion of faith.[2] We are thus still left with an initial element of faith which is something within man's power alone, but, as Origen declares that only complete faith can justify a man,[3] he is asserting that saving faith itself is not man's act alone but man's act rewarded and reinforced by the grace of God. Nevertheless, it has to be admitted that on this whole question of the nature of saving faith Origen is by no means consistent. In one passage of the Commentary on Romans he declares that complete faith, such as Abraham's was, *is* righteousness, so that when God reckons it as righteousness it is no fictitious imputation but rather a recognition of the reality of the case.[4] Yet only a very little later he goes on to declare that the fact that Abraham's faith was reckoned as righteousness while he was in uncircumcision emphasizes the truth that faith is reckoned as righteousness not for the righteous but for the unrighteous; otherwise it would lack the essential character of grace.[5]

Chrysostom does not follow the same line of argument at all. He regards the 'faith' of which I Cor. xii. 9 speaks as secondary and quite distinct from the basic usage of the word. It is a faith of σημεῖα, not of δόγματα, faith in a special sense which belongs to the context of the miraculous, not faith in the fundamental sense of Christian belief. It is a specific gift of Christ, but one cannot argue from it to the other kind of faith.[6] Nevertheless, his understanding of the subject must have been very similar to that of Origen. We have

---

[1] Origen on Rom. iv. 1–8 (Scherer, p. 182).

[2] Origen on Rom. iv. 18–22 (Scherer, pp. 212–14).

[3] Origen on Rom. iv. 1–8 (Scherer, p. 184; *J.T.S.* XIII, 357; *Comm. in Rom.* 4, 1 —963 B, C).

[4] Origen on Rom. iv. 1–8 (Scherer, p. 184). The relevant passage is admittedly incomplete, but the idea is fully consonant with Origen's views about the interrelatedness of all the virtues.

[5] Origen on Rom. iv. 9 (Scherer, p. 188).

[6] Chr. *Hom. in I Cor.* 29, 3 (10, 245). Cf. Cyr. Al. *Comm. in Joann.* xi. 40 (ed. Pusey, II, 285); but the attribution of this passage to Cyril is doubtful, and in Frag. on I Cor. xii. 9 (Pusey, p. 288) he interprets it rather as stability or faithfulness (ἑδραιότης). Chrysostom also claims that in Rom. xiv. 22–3 faith is used not in its basic sense περὶ δογμάτων but in a sense special to the context (*Hom. in Rom.* 26, 3—9, 640).

already seen that he regarded the desire to respond to God's act of liberation as a sphere of the joint operation of God and man. In commenting on the words of Paul in I Cor. iv. 7 'What hast thou that thou hast not received?', he cites faith as the first example of something received and says that it derives from the fact of our calling.[1] But he has no direct discussion of the issue comparable with that of Origen. In commenting, however, on the words of Phil. ii. 13, 'it is God who works in you both to will and to do', he interprets them to mean that if we will to will then God gives strength to our willing.[2] Just as with Origen's conception of faith, there is an essential initial element however small which lies within man's power; this, though inadequate in itself to achieve its goal, will be effectively reinforced by the grace of God. It is true that Chrysostom is here speaking not of the initial act of faith but of the continuing path of Christian living, but the structure of the two problems is similar. Origen indeed had pointed out in his own case that, since his understanding of faith in this connection derived from treating it as one of the gifts of the Spirit, his argument if valid at all must also apply to the other Christian virtues, which are without question gifts of the Spirit.[3] Certainly it is in connection with the Christian graces that Chrysostom speaks most clearly and confidently of the conjunction of the work of man and of God. Paul, he says, speaks of the *works* of the flesh because they are our doing alone, but of the *fruit* of the Spirit because that is the joint product of human and divine care.[4] All virtues are gifts of God, but gifts of a special kind, because they are not God's direct gifts but depend also on us. If Paul does not always mention the human element, it is in such cases as the gift of suffering for his name, where we are in danger of underestimating or ignoring altogether the divine side.[5] The correct balance involves explicit mention of both human achievement and divine working.[6] God gives the gift of the Spirit, but it is within

---

[1] Chr. *Hom. in I Cor.* 12, 2 (10, 98). Cf. *Hom. in Phil.* 11, 2 (11, 265) on Phil. iii. 9.

[2] Chr. *Hom. in Phil.* 8, 1 (11, 240).   [3] Origen, *Comm. in Joann.* Frag. 11.

[4] Chr. *Comm. in Gal.* 5, 6 (10, 673–4) on Gal. v. 22. Cf. Theod. *in loc.* (Swete, I, 101).

[5] Chr. *Hom. in Phil.* 4, 3 (11, 209) on Phil. i. 29. Unlike Origen, Chrysostom appears to take ἐχαρίσθη only with πάσχειν and not with πιστεύειν.

[6] Chr. *Hom. in Phil.* 1, 3 (11, 185–6) on Phil. i. 6.

our power to be filled with it or to quench it, as the Pauline imperatives imply.[1]

Certainly Chrysostom recognizes and seeks to do justice to the
prominent role of divine grace in Paul's thought. He sees Paul not
as a scholar concerned to propound a precise and systematic theology,
but as a missionary and pastor anxious to inculcate truly religious
attitudes in the lives of his people. It is to this motive that Paul's
vigorous stress on the divine initiative is to be traced. The systematic
theologian will have to re-express some of his assertions in a more
cautious and balanced form. But even then the grace of God is the
dominant theme. It is the sole and sufficient source of the originating
and objective element in man's redemption—the cross of Christ. It
is also to be recognized as playing an essential role as strengthening
and supplementing man's response of faith. Beyond this Chrysostom
cannot and will not go. A real place must be kept for the free
decision of man. If the love of God were to be elevated above the
rank of initiating cause and indispensable co-operating factor in the
work of man's salvation and were to be given the status of all-
sufficient cause, then, declares Chrysostom, there would be nothing
to prevent the automatic salvation of all.[2] I do not think that Paul
would have demurred.

When we turn to the writings of Augustine, we find him at first
holding a position similar to that of Theodore or Pelagius. In the
commentary on Romans, he declares firmly that the initial act of
faith is our act. God works all in all, but he does not believe all in
all.[3] Eighteen years later in the *De Spiritu et Litera* he expresses
himself more carefully and adopts a position not unlike that of
Chrysostom. He distinguishes the issue of initial faith from the
question of the subsequent Christian life and therefore refuses to use
Phil. ii. 13 in evidence. In the matter of faith, to will is open to us,

---

[1] Chr. *Hom. in Eph.* 19, 2 (11, 129) on Eph. v. 18; *Hom. in I Thess.* 11, 1 (11,
461) on I Thess. v. 19.

[2] Chr. *Hom. in Eph.* 1, 2 (11, 12) on Eph. i. 4–5. In one passage Origen even says
'Sic ergo non solum invitamur a deo, sed et trahimur et cogimur ad salutem' (*Hom.
in Num.* 20, 3). The words must not be interpreted so literally as to contradict the
general principle outlined in the text above, but they do show how very fully the
Eastern writers recognized the divine role at every point in the work of man's salvation.

[3] Augustine, *Expos. Prop. Ep. ad Rom.* 60 (Rom. ix. 11–13; I Cor. xii. 6).

but the effective power must come, as all power comes, from God. If we ask where the willing comes from, we cannot in spite of I Cor. iv. 7 say that it comes direct from God; to do so would be to make God responsible for sinners. But nor does it come entirely from us. In the first place free-will itself is God's gift.[1] Then God calls us both by preaching and by what comes into our minds. Our part is simply to give or to withhold assent. This does not invalidate the claim of I Cor. iv. 7 that we have nothing that we have not received. Faith is not a thing but the act of receiving; it is a matter of simple logic that the act of receiving must belong to the recipient rather than to the giver.[2] But twelve years later in the *Retractationes* his position has changed again. Faith is not to be treated differently from the other virtues. As Eph. vi. 23 suggests, it is on a par with love. It may still be called ours because of free-will, but it is also fully the gift of God. As Paul's words in I Cor. vii. 25 that he is one who has received mercy *to* be faithful imply, it is the outcome and not simply the condition of God's mercy.[3] Augustine develops this final position more fully in the *De Gratia et Libero Arbitrio* and the *De Praedestinatione Sanctorum*. The context in which the key text, I Cor. iv. 7, occurs in Paul's letters shows, Augustine argues, that it must be applied to the initial act of faith.[4] In fact a vast catena of Pauline texts is produced to show both negatively man's insufficiency to muster faith for himself and positively that faith is to be understood as a gift of God.[5] Augustine's argument may be summarized in two distinct ways. At times he is concerned simply to argue that there is no distinctive separable act of faith which is altogether ours and not God's. In this respect he is a true interpreter of Paul, avoiding the great pitfall of turning the Pauline conception of faith into yet another peculiar kind of work. But at times he goes further and seems to describe faith as a purely divine act effected

---

[1] This point had been made by Origen in a similar context (*De Principiis*, 3, 1, 19 with reference to Phil. ii. 13). Cf. Jerome on Eph. ii. 8 (470 B), which also comes evidently from Origen.

[2] *De Spir. et Lit.* XXXI, 53–4; XXXIII, 57–XXXIV, 60.

[3] *Retractationes*, I, 23, 2–4.   [4] *De Praed. Sanct.* IV, 8–V, 10.

[5] *De Grat. et Lib. Arb.* VII, 16–18; XIV, 28; *De Praed. Sanct.* II, 3–VIII, 16. The main Pauline texts used are Rom. iv. 21, xi. 35, xii. 3, I Cor. iv. 7, vii. 25, II Cor. iii. 5, iv. 13, Eph. ii. 8, vi. 23, Phil. i. 29, II Thess. iii. 2.

altogether apart from us. Here also there are elements in Paul's letters which might seem to support him. But it has to be admitted that his attempts to overcome the broader objections raised by all the Greek theologians and even by himself in his earlier years cannot be counted to have been very successful.

But the most important aspect of Augustine's contribution to this whole subject should not be regarded as his readiness to go that bit further than Chrysostom in unqualified affirmation of the absolute priority of divine grace. It is to be seen rather in something altogether different—his recognition that Paul is concerned more with the freedom to which the Christian is brought than with the philosophical concept of free-will. This was not of course an entirely new idea. But for the most part the Greek Fathers overlook this aspect of the question.[1] Augustine begins at least to restore to it a proper emphasis. Before grace, man is the slave of sin; the only freedom at that stage with which Paul is concerned is the freedom to believe, not the freedom to live without sin in one's own strength.[2] But more important still is the freedom open to the man under grace; it is where the Spirit of the Lord is that there is true liberty.[3] This does not remove the earlier problems altogether, but it helps to reduce them to their proper proportion in the work of Pauline exegesis by opening up a whole new aspect of the question of human freedom.

[1] Clement perhaps comes nearest to it in his conception of the true Gnostic's freedom from desire, but the idea is not linked very closely by him with Pauline exegesis.

[2] *Expos. Prop. Ep. ad Rom.* 44 (Rom. vii. 19–20).

[3] *De Spir. et Lit.* xxx, 52 (II Cor. iii. 17). On this whole question, cf. K. H. Schelkle, *Paulus Lehrer der Väter*, pp. 439–40.

CHAPTER VII

FAITH AND WORKS

The tradition of Greek theology, as we have seen, emphasizes and even exaggerates the importance of the free response of man in Paul's thought. The basic word for speaking of that response is faith. But whether subsequent interpreters understood that word in exactly the same sense as Paul did is a matter open to serious question. There is a clear and radical difference of spirit between the ways in which Paul and Origen speak about faith. For Paul faith is a glorious reality and he is its enthusiastic champion. For Origen, even when he seeks to be Paul's interpreter, it is rather a regrettable necessity and he is its cautious and conscientious apologist. Faith is not the ideal or natural way for man to come to God. It would have been far better for him to have come by the way of wisdom. It is only because man has failed to achieve that better way that God in his condescension has opened up for man the secondary and inferior way of faith.[1] On one occasion Paul does contrast faith with sight to the apparent detriment of the former. Origen interprets this contrast not in terms of the limitations of the present life as compared with the life to come, but in terms of differing grades of Christians. In an interesting passage of the commentary on St John he distinguishes with the aid of a number of Pauline texts three types of people: those who are 'in the flesh' (ἐν σαρκί), who war according to the flesh and who cannot please God, those who are 'in the body' (ἐν σώματι), who walk by faith and do not recognize the spiritual meaning of Scripture, and those who are truly spiritual, who walk not by faith but by sight.[2] Faith is here the characteristic mark of the weaker brother.

Moreover, where Paul speaks of the role and efficacy of faith in unqualified and all-embracing terms, Origen introduces certain restrictions and qualifications into the range of its working. These

[1] *Con. Cel.* 1, 13 (I Cor. i. 21). Cf. also the references given in p. 105 n. 2, above.
[2] *Comm. in Joann.* 13, 53 (Rom. viii. 8; II Cor. v. 7).

qualifications are sometimes but by no means always given a grounding in the words of Paul. When commenting on Paul's emphatic assertion that justification is by faith apart from works of the law, Origen is careful to restrict the application of the words to the forgiveness of past sins only.[1] Fornication before conversion can be forgiven on repentance; after conversion it cannot be so forgiven, though it can be 'covered' by good works.[2] Such ideas clearly give to the concept of works a significant role in the matter of man's justi-fication. The precise nature of that role needs careful consideration.

Works done without faith cannot justify a man; they may rightly be allowed, Origen says, to carry a certain honour and glory with them, but they cannot bring a man to eternal life or secure him membership of the kingdom of heaven.[3] On this point Origen is at one with all the early commentators.[4] Ambrosiaster in particular emphasizes that natural righteousness gives only a *temporis justitia* and that faith must be added to give an *aeternitatis justitia*.[5] But the case is very different with works which follow a man's entry upon the way of faith. The Christian who has faith certainly escapes judgement on the basic question of belief; but he has still to undergo a judgement on the basis of his works.[6] Origen insists that in Rom. ii Paul quite clearly enunciates the principle of judgement by works, and this, he says, excludes not only the heretical belief in fixed natures but also the view to be found among the faithful that faith alone is sufficient.[7] Origen is quite clear that when Paul speaks of

---

[1] Origen on Rom. iii. 28 (Scherer, p. 164; *Comm. in Rom.* 3, 9—953 C).

[2] Origen, Frag. on I Cor. v. 9–11 (*J.T.S.* IX, 366). The distinction is based on the wording of Ps. xxxii. 1 quoted in Rom. iv. 7–8. Cf. Origen on Rom. iv. 8 (Scherer, pp. 186–8—*J.T.S.* XIII, 358; *Comm. in Rom.* 4, 1—965 C, D).

[3] Origen, *Comm. in Rom.* 2, 7 (888 A, B) on Rom. ii. 10; on Rom. iii. 28 (Scherer, p. 166; *J.T.S.* XIII, 222).

[4] Cf. Clement, *Stromateis*, 1, 38, 1–2 (Rom. iv. 2); Apollinarius on Rom. ii. 13 (Staab, p. 60).

[5] Ambst. on Rom. ii. 12; iii. 20; iv. 2; Gal. iii. 12, 21 (67 B, 78 C, 82 B, 354 B, 357 D). Cf. his interpretation of the text 'While we have time let us do good unto all men' as meaning 'Now that we are Christians'; before a man is a Christian he has no opportunity of doing good (on Gal. vi. 10—370 D–371 A).

[6] Origen, *Comm. in Rom.* 2, 7 (889 A, B) on Rom. ii. 8–11.

[7] *Ibid.* 2, 4 (878 C, D) on Rom. ii. 6. The same point is much emphasized by Pelagius (on I Cor. vi. 9–10; Gal. v. 24; Eph. v. 5–6—pp. 155–6, 337–8, 373–4). Pelagius does frequently use the words 'faith alone' without any qualification (on

good works actually leading to eternal life itself, he must be addressing Christians and speaking about works which follow faith. He finds support for this view in Paul's use of the phrase 'patience in well-doing' (ὑπομονὴ ἔργου ἀγαθοῦ), which seems to him more appropriate if applied to specifically Christian well-doing.[1] Belief, even though it be belief in what is true, which is not strong enough to lead to good works is belief in vain.[2] It is not the mere reception of God's gift which saves the recipient but the persevering in worthy possession of it.[3] Some sins in the life of the Christian are 'not fitting' but do not lose the Christian his inheritance; others exclude him altogether from the kingdom of heaven.[4] The judgement upon his works may amount to assigning him a place with the unbelievers.[5] But over against this strand in Origen's teaching one has to set passages in which he asserts with apparently equal emphasis that faith alone saves, and quotes the examples of the penitent thief and the woman who was a sinner in Luke vii.[6] It is not easy to reconcile these statements. We might say that Origen appears to assert that faith without any ensuing works will save a man, whereas faith followed by evil works will not be reckoned as faith at all. No doubt there is an element of inconsistency in Origen's thought at this point, but the most significant fact is that at his best Origen is not really prepared to accept the problem at all in the precise form in which it is here posed. He asserts that, although Scripture does speak of a righteous man

---

Rom. v. 1; xi. 25; II Cor. v. 19; Gal. i. 3; i. 12; ii. 2; ii. 14; ii. 17; ii. 20; iii. 5; iii. 6; iii. 14; iii. 22; iii. 26; v. 11; vi. 16; Eph. ii. 8; ii. 16; iii. 11; Phil. iii. 3; iii. 9; iv. 1— pp. 41, 91, 261, 307, 309, 312, 315, 316, 317, 318, 318, 320, 322, 323, 334, 342, 353, 355, 359, 405, 407, 411), but it is clear from his more detailed statements that he regards it as a first step which is of no value apart from the subsequent works (on Rom. iii. 28; iv. 5; I Cor. ix. 21; Gal. iii. 10—pp. 34, 36, 178, 319).

[1] Origen, *Comm. in Rom.* 2, 7 (887 B) on Rom. ii. 7. The same insistence that those with whom Paul is concerned in Rom. ii are gentile *Christians* is strongly repeated by Ambrosiaster and by Augustine (Ambst. on Rom. ii. 14 (68 A); Augustine, *De Spir. et Lit.* XXVI, 43–XXVIII, 49; *Con. Jul. Pel.* 4, 3, 23–5).

[2] Origen, Frag. on I Cor. xv. 2 (*J.T.S.* x, 43).

[3] Origen, Frag. on I Cor. x. 5 (*J.T.S.* x, 29).

[4] Origen, Frag. on Eph. v. 3–5 (*J.T.S.* III, 559–60).

[5] Origen, *Comm. in Rom.* 2, 12 (900 A) on Rom. ii. 25. Cf. Frag. on Rom. iii. 28 (*J.T.S.* XIII, 222).

[6] Origen, *Comm. in Rom.* 3, 9 (952 C–953 B) on Rom. iii. 28.

turning away from his righteousness and committing iniquity, it never speaks of a man who has once believed and been justified turning away from his faith. Faith makes the promise sure in the sense that it imparts to the soul a kind of indelible and unalterable dye.[1] It is true that he is always prepared to insist very strongly on the absolute necessity of both faith and works; they are symbolized by the two circumcisions of the flesh and of the heart of which the prophets and Paul speak, and the two must go together.[2] But this is not just a listing of two distinct requirements for salvation; the two are organically linked. For all his insistence on the necessity of faith *and* works in the spirit, and sometimes in the very language of the Epistle of James,[3] it is clear that at the deepest level of his thought he does not really concede the existence of such a thing as faith without works; a faith which does not issue in works is not in the real meaning of the word faith at all.

The way in which Origen transposes the question into a new key is well illustrated by the nature of his comments on Rom. x. 9.[4] This text, he says, might suggest to some that faith without any good works is sufficient to save a man from destruction, even though it would have no power to bring him to a true glory. Indeed the language of Origen which we have studied so far might well lead us to expect that he would himself adopt such a conclusion. He does not in fact deny it, but he goes on in this way: 'consider whether it ought not rather to be understood like this—whoever truly confesses with his mouth Jesus as Lord and believes with his heart, let him similarly confess himself to be subject to the Lordship of wisdom and righteousness and truth and everything else which Christ is'. It is this second line of answer to the problem that is most distinctive of Origen. He develops it in a most thorough and forceful manner and it represents his fundamental resolution of the problem of the relation of faith and works.

Christ did not merely possess the various virtues accidentally or contingently; Christ *is* his attributes. This point is made clear not

---

[1] Origen on Rom. iv. 16–17 (Scherer, pp. 206–8; *J.T.S.* XIII, 360).

[2] *Comm. in Rom.* 2, 13 (908 B) on Rom. ii. 25–9.

[3] E.g. *Comm. in Joann.* 19, 23; *Comm. in Rom.* 2, 12 (900 A) on Rom. ii. 25 (Jas. ii. 26).

[4] *Comm. in Rom.* 8, 2 (1163 B, C). Cf. *Comm. in Matt.* 12, 24.

only by John but also by Paul, especially in I Cor. i. 30.[1] Therefore our relationship to Christ is automatically our relationship to wisdom, righteousness, truth and all the other virtues. To be 'in Christ' is to be 'in' all the virtues;[2] to have Christ in us is to have them in us.[3] To be 'in Christ' is the same as to serve him,[4] and to be his servant is to be the servant of all the virtues.[5] To put on Christ is to put on all the virtues, and conversely to put on the armour of God is to put on Christ.[6] Clearly therefore according to this analysis there can be for Origen no faith without works. Faith in Christ does not need to be supplemented by the virtuous life; it *is* the adoption of the virtues. Thus the connection between faith and works is a logically necessary one. If access to God is through Christ, then righteousness and truth are the gateway to God's presence, and it follows as a necessary deductive inference that 'the unrighteous cannot enter the kingdom of God'.[7] This point is well illustrated by Origen's penetrating interpretation of the opening verses of the sixth chapter of Romans. When Paul poses the question 'Shall we continue in sin that grace may abound?', the 'God forbid' (μὴ γένοιτο) with which he answers his own question is no substitute for reasoning but is followed by reasoning of logical cogency. Grace *can* only abound for those who have died to sin. The question of continuing in sin that grace may abound is not therefore a regrettable counsel to be opposed but a logical impossibility to be

---

[1] *Con. Cel.* 5, 39; *Comm. in Joann.* 1, 22; 1, 34; 6, 6; *Comm. in Rom.* 3, 7 (945 B, C) on Rom. iii. 24. Origen uses Eph. ii. 14 in the same way (Frag. *in loc. J.T.S.* III, 406; *Comm. in Joann.* 19, 23; 20, 37; 28, 18).

[2] Origen, Frags. on Eph. i. 3; iv. 32; vi. 10 (*J.T.S.* III, 236, 558, 570); *Comm. in Rom.* 5, 10 (1056A) on Rom. vi. 11; *ibid.* 10, 12 (1269A) on Rom. xv. 17. In commenting on Eph. iii. 12 (*J.T.S.* III, 409) Origen makes the point the other way round, namely that he who does everything by reason has believed in Christ the Logos, and similarly with wisdom, truth and righteousness.

[3] Origen, *Comm. in Rom.* 7, 9 (1129C) on Rom. viii. 32; Jerome on Gal. ii. 20 (345 C).

[4] Origen, *Comm. in Rom.* 6, 11 (1092A) on Rom. viii. 1.

[5] *Ibid.* 1, 1 (839C) on Rom. i. 1; *ibid.* 6, 5 (1065 C) on Rom. vi. 22; *ibid.* 10, 1 (1251B) on Rom. xiv. 18.

[6] *Ibid.* 9, 34 (1234B) on Rom. xiii. 14; Frag. on Eph. vi. 11 (*J.T.S.* III, 570). For an extensive list of similar examples drawn from the whole range of Origen's works see M. Harl, *Origène*, pp. 290–1.

[7] Origen on Rom. v. 2 (Scherer, p. 224—*Comm. in Rom.* 4, 8—990B); Frag. on I Cor. vi. 9 (*J.T.S.* IX, 368).

exposed.[1] This is the significance of the ensuing description of baptism. Paul describes baptism as being buried with Christ; but burial logically presupposes death. Baptism therefore that is not preceded by a moral dying with Christ is not really baptism at all.[2] Similarly, as he says in another baptismal context, we do not really believe in our heart that God has raised Christ from the dead unless he is risen and living in us in his capacity as the embodiment of all the virtues.[3]

The value of Origen's analysis may be brought out by a brief comparison with two of the Latin commentators, Victorinus and Pelagius. Victorinus speaks the language of direct personal communion. To live by faith in the Son of God is paraphrased as 'de ipso cogitare, ipsum loqui, ipsum credere, ad ipsum desiderio tendere'.[4] To be in Christ is defined in similar terms,[5] and to be baptized into Christ is to receive Christ and to be Christ.[6] Such language does full justice to the personal quality of faith in the thought of Paul, but it does not grapple at all with the problem of the relationship of that faith to works. At the other extreme Pelagius is content to reduce all such ideas to the concept of imitation. For him to have Christ in one is simply to imitate him.[7] Origen contrives to present in a unified form both these distinct emphases. He does present faith in terms of a truly personal relationship with Christ, but at the same time he safeguards the idea from any misunderstanding which by emphasizing its contrast with works might serve to undermine its moral force.

But his analysis does raise a further problem in an acute form. If

---

[1] *Comm. in Rom.* 5, 7 (1036A) on Rom. vi. 1–2.

[2] *Ibid.* 5, 8 (1038A) on Rom. vi. 3–4. In this passage Origen points out that, although Paul here speaks of Christians as 'consepulti' with Christ, he never speaks of them as 'conbaptizati'. Christ's baptism was the end of the old order rather than the beginning of the new. In the light of the modern tendency to stress Christian baptism as a 'representation of the Baptism of Jesus' (G. W. H. Lampe, *Seal of the Spirit* (1951), p. 45), the point is worth making.

[3] *Comm. in Rom.* 8, 2 (1163C) on Rom. x. 9. Cf. Origen on Rom. iv. 24 (Scherer, p. 222).

[4] Victorinus on Gal. ii. 20 (1166A, B).

[5] *Ibid.* on Phil. iii. 9 (1219C); on Eph. ii. 11 (1256C, D).

[6] *Ibid.* on Gal. iii. 27–9 (1173B–D).

[7] Pelagius on Rom. viii. 10 (p. 63).

to be 'in Christ', Paul's basic description of a Christian, means to live out all the virtues, then it would appear that only the perfect are to be regarded as Christians at all. But Origen is quite clear that this would be a false conclusion.[1] He is forced therefore to conclude that the concept of being 'in Christ' is not one which has always to be either wholly true or wholly false when applied to a particular person. It is possible to be 'partly in the flesh and partly in the spirit'. Being 'in Christ' is something that has to be progressively realized.[2] A man's character cannot be changed overnight; the conversion of the will may be immediate, but the development of the habit of consistently good actions is a slow and laborious business.[3] Both the dying with Christ and the rising to newness of life with him, which are the essential meaning of Christian baptism, are at the same time something in the past which happens once for all and something continuous which requires to be renewed daily. Moreover, that daily renewal is no mere continuation of the past experience but a developing process of growth. But even this twofold pattern of ideas does not constitute the full significance of our identification with Christ's death and resurrection through baptism. The process of growth has a goal of ultimate perfection; the concept of rising again with Christ points to the third notion of a final resurrection with him from death.[4] Origen points out that in I Cor. xv. 22 Paul uses neither past nor present but a future tense—'in Christ *shall* all be made alive'. This prompts him to suggest that dying with Christ is an appropriate description of the present age as a time of labour and work during which men may acquire merits through their good manner of life, and that this will lead on to a future life with Christ.[5]

Two points of interest are illustrated in this comment. In the first place the introduction of the category of merit is significant. This

---

[1] Origen, *Comm. in Rom.* 2, 7 (889 C) on Rom. ii. 8–11.

[2] *Ibid.* 6, 11 (1091 C–1092 A) on Rom. viii. 1–2. Cf. *Comm. in Joann.* 20, 34 (I Cor. xiii. 2, 9, 10); *De Principiis*, 4, 4, 2.

[3] *Comm. in Rom.* 6, 9 (1088 A, B) on Rom. vii. 18; *De Principiis*, 3, 1, 17. Cf. Diodore on Rom. xiii. 11 (Staab, p. 108).

[4] *Comm. in Rom.* 5, 8 (1042 A–C) on Rom. vi. 4; *ibid.* 5, 10 (1048 C–1049 A) on Rom. vi. 8–10.

[5] *Ibid.* 5, 1 (1006 A) on Rom. v. 12.

occurs frequently in Origen's writings, especially with reference to men deserving the grace of the Holy Spirit. Thus those who are in the spirit and not in the flesh are said to be those who by their deeds and manner of life have merited having the Spirit of God in them.[1] The concept of progress and growth in grace is undoubtedly present in Paul; as Origen clearly recognizes, there are for Paul those who are 'carnal' (σάρκινοι) and 'babes in Christ' (νήπιοι ἐν χριστῷ).[2] If Origen emphasizes the need for growth more than Paul, it is no more than a comparatively slight difference of emphasis. It is in his description of this progress and growth as an acquisition of merit that he appears to deviate more radically from the thought of Paul. In this respect, however, he is at one with almost all other early commentators. Once again Victorinus stands out as something of an exception, and it is instructive to compare his exegesis of Phil. iii. 13–14 with that of Ambrosiaster. According to Victorinus, Paul forgets what is behind because to remember one's past (even one's good deeds) is to rely on works rather than on grace; according to Ambrosiaster he forgets what is behind because, though not actually bad, it was of no great merit towards the winning of a future reward.[3] But a word of caution is needed before Origen is simply condemned outright on the strength of such language as deserting altogether the Pauline doctrine of grace and replacing it with an alien doctrine of merit. In the first place a very large number of the most striking examples of Origen's use of merit language occur in works existing only in Latin translations. Moreover, even if the translator has been reasonably faithful at these points, the Latin words 'mereri' and 'meritum' carry a stronger implication of 'merit' than the original Greek words which they represent.[4] The basic

---

[1] *Comm. in Rom.* 6, 12 (1096 C) on Rom. viii. 9. An extensive list of examples of this kind from Origen's writings is given in B. Drewery, *Origen and the Doctrine of Grace* (1960), pp. 193–4.

[2] Frag. on I Cor. iii. 1 (*J.T.S.* IX, 241). Origen emphasizes that not only νήπιοι but also σάρκινοι is to be taken with ἐν χριστῷ. This is in line with the exegesis of Clement, who understands the σάρκινοι and νήπιοι ἐν χριστῷ as unbaptized catechumens and the πνευματικοί as those who have received the Spirit in baptism (*Paidagogos*, 1, 36, 2–3).   [3] Victorinus, *in loc.* (1222 B); Ambst. *in loc.* (416 D).

[4] Cf. B. Drewery (*op. cit.* pp. 205–6), who writes 'I think I could demonstrate in detail how his Latin translators heighten the element of merit beyond his intentions'.

terms which Origen himself uses are ἄξιος and καταξιῶμαι. On at least three occasions in the New Testament itself those words are used of man's relation to his final heavenly reward.[1] If the concept of growth in grace has any meaning at all, it must mean that the faithful reception of God's gifts makes us able or fit to receive his further gifts; to him that hath shall be given. Origen himself makes this point explicitly. 'The measure of the gift of Christ' according to which grace is given to every man is, he says, a matter of our capacity to receive it; any withholding of grace has only the purpose of sparing the recipients who could not receive it beneficially.[2] A fair proportion of Origen's ἄξιος-language in its original intention need imply no more than that. On the other hand it must be admitted that on occasions Origen certainly does speak of the merit of our own achievements as something apparently wholly distinct from the God-given grace of the Holy Spirit. But, however much we are forced to admit the presence of this idea of merit in the thought of Origen, it was certainly not intended to imply an exact equivalence of desert and reward. The principle that with what measure ye mete it shall be measured to you again applies, he insists, only to our evil deeds; the 'reward' of our good deeds always exceeds our deserving. That is the deliberate reason why Paul carefully speaks in Rom. vi. 23 of death as the *wages* of sin, but of eternal life as being the *gift* of God.[3] Diodore similarly points out that Paul describes the ultimate glory as incomparably greater than the faithful suffering that must precede it; it is therefore not a matter of mere compensation or reward, it is still a matter of God's grace.[4] Augustine also seeks to show in a different way that the idea of merited reward is not incompatible with the basic idea of grace. In accepting the implication of Rom. ii that good works lead to heaven, he is careful to add that the works are themselves the gift of God's grace.[5]

---

[1] Rev. iii. 4; Luke xx. 35; II Thess. i. 5.

[2] Origen, Frag. on Eph. iv. 7 (*J.T.S.* III, 413).

[3] Origen on Rom. iv. 1–8 (Scherer, pp. 184–6; *J.T.S.* XIII, 358; *Comm. in Rom.* 4, 1—964 B).

[4] Diodore on Rom. viii. 17–18 (Staab, p. 93).

[5] Augustine, *De Grat. et Lib. Arb.* VII, 17; *Ep.* 186, 4 (Rom. ii. 6). This point is emphasized by G. Nygren as illustrative both of the similarity and of the difference

The second point of interest in Origen's description of the present as a time of dying with Christ and the future as one of living with him lies in its clear emphasis on the superiority of the future world. Paul appears to lay an almost equal emphasis upon the completeness of Christ's gifts to the believer now and upon the even greater nature of those that lie in the future. Origen clearly recognizes this double emphasis. He points out that Paul speaks regularly of the Christian's resurrection both as a present spiritual reality and as a more literal future event.[1] He even regards a present spiritual interpretation of the idea that the Christian has been made to sit down in heavenly places with Christ as more profound than a future interpretation.[2] Yet he is consciously puzzled by texts which speak of ordinary Christians as already possessing or likely to possess a wholeness of wisdom and knowledge. He does admit that anyone who truly believes and thereby has the Holy Spirit has a fullness of God's gifts.[3] Indeed the very fact of God's gift of the Spirit involves treating us as if we had been already and all at once made perfect.[4] But he prefers in his exegesis to bring out more clearly the incompleteness of the Christian's present position. Thus the 'all wisdom and all knowledge' of which Paul speaks in Eph. i. 9 are not to be regarded as unqualified concepts. They refer only to the theme of forgiveness or the economy of man's salvation, but leave over to the future the realm of the 'great mysteries' (τὰ ἀπόρρητα).[5] Or again the use of the word 'all' may be regarded as comparative; as compared with ordinary human goodness or knowledge the Christian has the whole; as compared with God's perfection such

---

between the Augustinian and the Pauline conceptions of the relation between grace and salvation (G. Nygren, 'The Augustinian Conception of Grace', *Studia Patristica*, II, 266–8).

[1] Origen, Frag. on Rom. vi. 5 (*J.T.S.* XIII, 363–4; *Comm. in Rom.* 5, 9—1047 C–1048 A). Cf. Ambst. on Col. iii. 1 (434 A).

[2] Origen, Frag. on Eph. ii. 6 (*J.T.S.* III, 405); Jerome, *in loc.* (468 B–469 A). Cf. also Origen, Frag. on Eph. i. 22 (*J.T.S.* III, 401).

[3] Origen, *Comm. in Rom.* 10, 9 (1265 B, C) on Rom. xv. 13.

[4] *Ibid.* 7, 2 (1105 C) on Rom. viii. 15.

[5] Frag. on Eph. i. 9 (*J.T.S.* III, 240). According to Origen two punctuations of the passage are possible. Either the words are to be taken with the preceding verse about forgiveness or their interpretation is to be closely linked with and controlled by the word μυστήριον.

goodness and knowledge are at best partial.[1] Now we see dimly, then face to face.[2] Now we have only the 'form' (τύπος) of doctrine, then we shall have the doctrine itself.[3] The *reign* of righteousness and Paul's great affirmation that there is 'no condemnation for those who are in Christ Jesus' are to be understood to refer to a future time of perfection.[4] We live in hope of the glory of God and therefore even though we have already been shown the glory 'as of the only begotten' there must be an even greater 'glory of the Father' which still lies in the future.[5] Thus as an exegete he does seriously seek to take cognizance of the two sides of Paul's thought. But he does not find it easy to do full justice to those texts which speak most strongly of the Christian's enjoyment of God's gifts already in this present world. The emphasis in his own thinking at this point is undoubtedly conditioned by the stress on the transience and the imperfection of this world which characterized the Platonist tradition in which he stood. While he does not accept without qualification Celsus' assertion that 'error is associated with becoming', yet he is relieved to be able to claim that the important sense in which such a statement is true finds full expression in Paul's writings.[6] The Christian still lives in the realm of shadow; his life is Christ, but it is still hidden; he is still absent from his Lord.[7] The focus of Paul's gospel as Origen interprets it lies in the future rather than in the past or the present.

This future emphasis in the interpretation of Paul's teaching about faith and justification is very much more marked in the writings of Theodore. For Theodore, as we have seen, the root problem of man's life is the problem of his mortality. Therefore the fundamental answer to man's problem must necessarily lie in the future.[8] The word 'salvation' in Rom. xiii. 11 means resurrection, because that

---

[1] *Comm. in Rom.* 10, 10 (1266 B) on Rom. xv. 14.

[2] I Cor. xiii. 12 is a favourite text with Origen. In *De Oratione*, 11, 2 he claims that, while in its original context it refers only to knowledge, it is by analogy true of all the virtues.

[3] Origen, *Comm. in Rom.* 6, 3 (1061 C, D) on Rom. vi. 16.

[4] *Ibid.* 5, 3 (1028 A, B) on Rom. v. 17; *ibid.* 6, 11 (1092 B, C) on Rom. viii. 1.

[5] Origen on Rom. v. 2 (Scherer, pp. 228–30; *Comm. in Rom.* 4, 8—991–2).

[6] *Con. Cel.* 7, 50 (I Cor. xiii. 12; II Cor. v. 5–6).

[7] *Dial. Herac.*, ed. Scherer, p. 174 (Col. iii. 3–4; II Cor. v. 6, 8).

[8] See p. 63 above.

is the 'ultimate salvation' (ἀληθινὴ σωτηρία).[1] The 'justification of life' (δικαίωσις ζωῆς) with which Christ replaces the sin of Adam is the sinlessness of the future life;[2] so more strikingly still is the redemption, the forgiveness of our sins which we have in him.[3] Adoption as sons of God is the future resurrection which is the Christian's destiny.[4] The idea of faith has a necessarily future reference implying belief in something we do not yet possess, and is closely akin to the concepts of promise and of hope.[5] Such teaching is most clearly evident in the Epistle to the Ephesians with its references to the heavenly places and the ages to come,[6] but Theodore insists that it is the universal teaching of Paul in all his epistles.[7] Baptism represents the moment of transference to this resurrection life, but it is a transference not in full reality but 'at the level of prefigurative symbol' (κατὰ τύπον).[8] It is true that baptism does at the same time impart the first-fruits of the Spirit, but Theodore is insistent that the real evidence to justify Paul's theological assertions cannot be found in present experience but only in the future.[9] It is the new status as something received κατὰ τύπον in baptism and pointing forward to its future realization rather than the first-fruits of the Spirit as a present possession that is primary in the thought of Theodore. This is clearly evidenced by his relation of the concept of works to faith and baptism. The basic idea is one of fittingness. Having received the Spirit as a promise of immortality, it is only fitting and right that the Christian should live a life consistent with the idea of immortal life.[10] Full perfection cannot be expected in this life, but the nearest

---

[1] Theod. *in loc.* (Staab, p. 163).

[2] Theod. on Rom. v. 18 (Staab, p. 120).

[3] *Ibid.* on Col. i. 14 (Swete, I, 261).

[4] *Ibid.* on Gal. iii. 26 (Swete, I, 55–6); on Rom. viii. 15 (Staab, p. 136).

[5] *Ibid.* on Gal. iii. 23; Eph. i. 4, 12; Col. i. 27 (Swete, I, 52, 123, 131, 281).

[6] *Ibid.* on Eph. i. 3; ii. 6–7 (Swete, I, 121–2, 145–6).

[7] *Ibid.* on Col. i. 22 (Swete, I, 278).

[8] *Ibid.* on Gal. ii. 15–16 (Swete, I, 30; Theodore's comments on these verses contain his fullest treatment of this whole subject in the commentaries); on Gal. ii. 20; iii. 27–8; v. 24; Eph. iv. 22–4; Col. ii. 12; ii. 14 (Swete, I, 34, 58, 102, 173–4, 288, 290–1); on Rom. vi. 17 (Staab, p. 123); *Cat. Hom.* 14, 5–6.

[9] Theod. on Eph. ii. 7 (Swete, I, 146).

[10] *Ibid.* on Gal. v. 16; Eph. iv. 22–4; Phil. iii. 15; Col. iii. 6 (Swete, I, 98, 174, 239–40, 300); on Rom. vi. 3; vi. 12–14; xiii. 14 (Staab, pp. 121, 122, 164).

approach to it that lies within our powers is demanded.[1] A bad Christian life may lead to a lesser fulfilment of the Spirit's promise or in the extreme case to its loss altogether.[2] Thus Theodore's whole account of faith and of justification is dominated by his understanding of death as the root evil to be overcome.

Chrysostom's writings provide a more general consideration of the nature of faith and one which provides an instructive contrast to that of Origen. For Chrysostom faith is no secondary or tertiary virtue; the faith which is ranked after wisdom and knowledge in the list of the Spirit's gifts is not the basic saving faith with which Paul is primarily concerned.[3] Chrysostom's approach therefore has a positive ring about it which is missing in the thought of Origen. For him it seems natural to contrast faith not to its detriment with wisdom, knowledge or sight, but to its advantage with ratiocination (λογισμοί). It is not an inferior alternative means of approach made necessary by man's failure and man's sin; it is the means appropriate to the nature of its object. Ratiocination can never take us the whole way; it can for example tell us certain things about the ability to see and hear, but it cannot deal with the fundamental question of how the eye sees or the ear hears. So the divine realm lies beyond the range of ratiocination, and faith is the appropriate means by which it must be apprehended.[4] The resurrection of Christ may have partial analogies in earlier risings from the dead, but they are only partial because they were risings to die again; the virgin-birth has no analogies. They cannot therefore be reached by a process of argument; faith alone is adequate to such an object.[5]

If Chrysostom stands nearer to Paul in the positive nature of his attitude towards the idea of faith, his understanding of its real nature seems further removed from that of the apostle. The sense of personal union with Christ is largely absent. An intellectualist

[1] *Ibid.* on Gal. v. 16; Eph. iv. 22–4; I Thess. iv. 7 (Swete, I, 98, 174, II, 24); on Rom. vi. 12–14 (Staab, p. 122).

[2] *Ibid.* on I Thess. v. 23 (Swete, II, 40); on I Cor. v. 5 (Staab, p. 178).

[3] See p. 106 above.

[4] Chr. *Hom. in I Cor.* 4, 1 (10, 31) on I Cor. i. 18–20; *Hom. in Rom.* 1, 3 (9, 398) on Rom. i. 5; *ibid.* 17, 2 (9, 566) on Rom. x. 6–9. It is significant that Chrysostom regards Heb. xi as Paul's main treatment of the subject of faith (*Hom. in Eph.* 24, 2 on Eph. vi. 16—11, 170–1).

[5] Chr. *Hom. in Phil.* 11, 2 (11, 265–6) on Phil. iii. 9.

analysis in terms of the acceptance of basic dogma takes its place. This is implicit in the very phrase—πίστις τῶν δογμάτων—which he uses to distinguish it from other uses of the word.[1] It is therefore natural that by way of compensation he should lay even greater stress on the need of works to supplement the basis of faith.[2] Faith in this respect is treated on an exact par with baptism.[3] Together they constitute the initial saving event, but they must be followed by a consistent life of virtue. Both are equally necessary. Isaac was distinguished from Ishmael by the manner of his birth, and shows the need for the new birth from God; Israel was identical with Esau in the manner of his birth but was (according to Chrysostom) distinguished from him by the manner of life which God foresaw, and thus exemplifies the need for the life of virtue.[4] The Christian must be both 'holy' (ἅγιος), which implies having faith, and 'without blemish' (ἄμωμος), which implies living a blameless life.[5] It is on this second aspect, the essentiality of the subsequent life of good works, that the stress of Chrysostom the homilist in general lies.

The most striking exceptions occur in the commentary on Colossians. Just as it is there that an emphasis on the priority of God's act in the whole work of salvation, extending even to man's response of faith, is especially to be found, so also it is in the same writing that we find a reiterated insistence that the initial entry upon discipleship, the essence of the divine dispensation, the heart of the mystery, is to be found in faith, or in faith and baptism, alone, quite apart from all questions of virtue or good works.[6] He does not

---

[1] See p. 106 above. Chrysostom interprets δόγμασιν in Eph. ii. 15 and Col. ii. 14 as meaning faith (*Hom. in Eph.* 5, 2—11, 39; *Hom. in Col.* 6, 2—11, 340). Similarly he distinguishes the righteousness which is through Christ and the righteousness which is not according to Christ as signifying the good life μετὰ τῶν δογμάτων and the good life alone (*Hom. in Phil.* 2, 1 on Phil. i. 11—11, 191).

[2] Chr. *Hom. in Rom.* 5, 3 (9, 425) on Rom. ii. 7; *ibid.* 13, 7 (9, 517) on Rom. viii. 7; *ibid.* 29, 2 (9, 655) on Rom. xv. 16; *Hom. in I Cor.* 23, 1—2 (10, 190) on I Cor. ix. 27; *Hom. in II Cor.* 2, 1 (10, 392) on II Cor. i. 6; *Hom. in Eph.* 4, 3 (11, 34) on Eph. ii. 10; *Hom. in Phil.* 11, 2 (11, 266) on Phil. iii. 9.

[3] *Hom. in Rom.* 13, 5—6 (9, 515) on Rom. viii. 4; *ibid.* 14, 2 (9, 525) on Rom. viii. 14; *Hom. in I Cor.* 23, 2 (10, 191) on I Cor. x. 1—5.

[4] *Hom. in Rom.* 16, 6 (9, 556—7) on Rom. ix. 7—12.

[5] *Hom. in Eph.* 1, 2 (11, 12) on Eph. i. 4.

[6] *Hom. in Col.* 1, 1 (11, 301) on Col. i. 2; *ibid.* 4, 2 (11, 327) on Col. i. 25; *ibid.* 5, 1 (11, 332) on Col. i. 27.

present the two as necessarily and organically linked in quite the way that Origen does. His most characteristic understanding of their relation is that in faith and baptism there occurs a change not of φύσις but of προαίρεσις, a change not of nature but of ruling purpose. This does not mean that a life of good works must logically or automatically ensue; all that baptism stands for can in fact be lost again.[1] But the real change of ruling purpose effected there does make a difference; it does not guarantee a life of virtue, but it makes it εὔκολον, something easily to be achieved, something which in Paul's phrase needs only to be put on.[2] Chrysostom takes seriously both Paul's indicatives and his imperatives, both his assertions about the significance of baptism and his calls to moral endeavour. The Christian has put on the new man in his baptism but he has still to do so in life and works.[3] The Christian has been buried with Christ, but he has still to mortify his members upon the earth. These two ideas may appear contradictory but in reality they are not. The sculptor wipes all dirt off his statue when first he creates it, but there is nothing contradictory about his repeating the process later if rust begins to appear.[4] Sin died at our baptism so that the way to the good life lies wide open, but we can bring sin to life again.[5] The ultimate outcome of sin after conversion is final and irrevocable death.[6] The foundation upon which men build is Christ, and in this respect of fundamental faith there are no distinctions. But the different buildings that men raise are the differing actions and lives that follow, and here there is endless variety of quality. Those whose lives prove worthless are according to Paul 'saved as by fire'; but this does not mean that their bare faith allows them entry into the lowest mansion of heaven; rather it means that they are preserved alive in the eternal torments of fire.[7]

---

[1] *Comm. in Gal.* 4, 2 (10, 660) on Gal. iv. 19.
[2] *Hom. in Rom.* 11, 2 (9, 486) on Rom. vi. 12; *ibid.* 13, 8 (9, 519) on Rom. viii. 10; *Hom. in Col.* 8, 1 (11, 352-3) on Col. iii. 9-10; *ibid.* 8, 2 (11, 353) on Col. iii. 12.
[3] *Hom. in Eph.* 13, 2 (11, 96) on Eph. iv. 22-4.
[4] *Hom. in Col.* 8, 1 (11, 351) on Col. iii. 5.
[5] *Hom. in Rom.* 10, 4 (9, 479) on Rom. vi. 2; *Comm. in Gal.* 2, 8 (10, 646) on Gal. ii. 20.
[6] *Hom. in Rom.* 11, 4 (9, 488-9) on Rom. vi. 16.
[7] *Hom. in I Cor.* 9, 3 (10, 78-9) on I Cor. iii. 12-15.

The Christian is essentially still in pilgrimage. It is true that he has the earnest of the Spirit on the strength of his faith, but the full gift must await the completion of a life of good works.[1] Some of God's gifts he possesses already, and the list is no mean one—separation from sin, a new obedience to the way of righteousness, sanctification and the attainment of eternal life. But still more rests in the future.[2] Yet that which lies in the future is in another sense already realized. So Paul frequently ascribes to us what is true of Christ. It is the truth, though at present it is a hidden truth.[3] The final glory is not so much an addition as an unveiling of what is already true; it is an ἀποκάλυψις,[4] an ἀπολύτρωσις, for which we wait. But there is a further force in the ἀπο of ἀπολύτρωσις; it implies a completeness from which there can be no falling away. The λύτρωσις which is experienced already in this life is a reality but it can be lost; the ultimate ἀπολύτρωσις is eternal and irremissible.[5]

The man of faith is a pilgrim; he is a man still journeying towards the holy land. The quality of life which he shows forth in the course of that journey is a matter of the utmost importance. With this basic account all Paul's interpreters would agree. What rules or precepts then are given to him to guide him on his journey? What place has law in the life of the Christian?

To this question it is Theodore who offers the most radical answer. The Christian is the man who by baptism has entered upon the resurrection life; his life needs therefore to be lived according to the pattern of the heavenly life. In the life of heaven there is no place for circumcision, and it is for this reason that it is irrelevant to the Christian.[6] It is for the same reason that the distinctions of male and female, Jew and Greek, bond and free, are all done away in Christ.[7] Sometimes indeed Theodore appears to speak as if law itself has no place in the life of heaven and therefore no

---

[1] *Hom. in Eph.* 2, 2 (11, 18–19) on Eph. i. 14.

[2] *Hom. in Rom.* 12, 1–2 (9, 495–6) on Rom. vi. 22.

[3] *Hom. in Col.* 7, 2 (11, 345–6) on Col. iii. 3–4.

[4] *Hom. in Rom.* 14, 4 (9, 529) on Rom. viii. 18.

[5] *Ibid.* 14, 6 (9, 531) on Rom. viii. 23.

[6] Theod. on Gal. i. 1; Eph. ii. 14; Col. iii. 11 (Swete, I, 4, 150, 302). Cf. Jerome on Gal. vi. 15 (436B–437A).

[7] Theod. on Gal. iii. 28 (Swete, I, 57).

place in the life of the Christian.[1] But this judgement he modifies on two scores. In the first place the Christian has not yet wholly entered upon the resurrection life; he is not yet free from the shackles of mortality; he is a creature of two worlds in a kind of midway position belonging both to the present and to the future. He is therefore at the same time free from law and in need of it. His freedom from it is not yet complete and unqualified.[2] In the second place the law that has no place in the life of heaven is not the law absolutely. It is the specific positive precepts of the law that have no place; the moral precepts, when understood as an expression of love, have a place there and therefore have a place also in the life of the Christian.[3] Strictly speaking love is the only virtue that continues into the future life; it is therefore the law of Christ, it is therefore the central theme of all Paul's moral exhortation; but for its implementation in this life other subsidiary virtues may usefully be listed after it, and Paul's moral exhortation needs to take the form of specific counsels for harmony and concord.[4]

Other writers tend to have less hesitation in giving a definite place to rules and precepts in Christian life. Origen is typical in declaring that, as Moses gave the first law to those who had come out of Egypt and were beginning their journey to the holy land, so Christ has given the second law for the Christian pilgrim.[5] Paul therefore, he claims, in setting out a series of moral precepts is anxious to make clear that they are a part of God's gracious gift to mankind. Origen indeed suggests that the link of thought between chs. xii and xiii of Romans is that, while Gentiles are inclined to ascribe moral rules to the glory of their rulers, Christians ascribe them to God and to the Holy Spirit.[6] On occasion he seeks to spiritualize some of Paul's injunctions on the ground that their more obvious meaning is either platitudinous,[7] absurd[8] or irrelevant

---

[1] *Ibid.* on Gal. i. 4; iv. 30 (Swete, I, 8, 86); on Rom. vii. 6 (Staab, pp. 125–6).
[2] *Ibid.* on Gal. iii. 20; v. 25 (Swete, I, 49, 102).
[3] *Ibid.* on Gal. ii. 15–16 (Swete, I, 30–1).
[4] *Ibid.* on Gal. v. 22–3; vi. 2; Eph. iv. 1–3 (Swete, I, 100–1, 103–4, 163–4).
[5] Origen, *Con. Cel.* 2, 75.
[6] Origen, *Comm. in Rom.* 9, 24 (1225 C–1226 A) on Rom. xii. 1–21.
[7] Origen, Frag. on Eph. iv. 25 (*J.T.S.* III, 419).
[8] Origen, Frag. on Eph. iv. 26 (*J.T.S.* III, 420).

to the context.[1] These spiritualizations continue to recur in later writers, even in those of a less generally allegorical turn of mind.[2] More often, however, he is content to interpret them as straightforward moral teaching and uses Stoic definitions and biblical examples to bring out their particular force.[3]

One characteristic of particular importance about the moral rules given by Paul was very widely noted at an early stage. Those rules are intended to help the Christian pilgrim on his journey; they are therefore graded to suit men at the different stages of their advancement along that road. The principle which Christ ascribed to the Mosaic law of framing its demands in the light of the hardness of men's hearts is to be seen continued in the pronouncements of Paul.[4] A church whose members are largely children in the faith will not be faced with the full Christian demand.[5] Some commands are an essential part of our salvation, others are matters left to the freedom of our choice.[6] Paul clearly declares that some things are lawful but not profitable, and therefore, Tertullian concludes, not good. Paul's right to live by the gospel, the apostles' right to lead their wives about with them, the man's right to marry his virgin—these are all rights but they are better forgone.[7] Thus the pattern of Christian morality is regarded as that of a carefully graded hierarchy of demand, adapted to the spiritual capacity of each person.

Three points need to be noted about the exegetical basis of this line of thought, so important in the whole subsequent history of the 'double standard' of morality. First of all, it is not the private conception of any individual or small group; the idea is widespread at the earliest stage of the literary tradition. Secondly, its basis is to be seen very largely in the one letter of I Corinthians, as the refer-

---

[1] Origen, Frag. on I Cor. vii. 18–20 (*J.T.S.* IX, 506–7); *Comm. in Rom.* I, I (838 B, C) on Rom. i. 1; Jerome on Gal. v. 15 (410 B, C).

[2] E.g. Pelagius on Eph. iv. 26 (p. 370).

[3] Origen, Frags. on Eph. iv. 18, 26, 30, 31 (*J.T.S.* III, 416, 420, 555, 556).

[4] Irenaeus, *Adv. Haer.* 4, 15, 2 (Harvey, II, 188) (I Cor. vii. 5); Clement, *Stromateis*, 3, 82, 4 (I Cor. vii. 9).

[5] Tertullian, *De Monogamia*, 11, 6 (I Cor. iii. 2; vii. 1–2).

[6] Origen, Frag. on I Cor. vii. 25 (*J.T.S.* IX, 508–9).

[7] Tertullian, *Exhort. Cast.* 8, 1; Clement, *Stromateis*, 4, 149, 1–2 (I Cor. vii. 38); Origen, Frag. on I Cor. vi. 12 (*J.T.S.* IX, 369–70—I Cor. ix. 4, 9–18; ix. 5; vii. 32–8).

ences given above clearly reveal. Matthew xix. 21, the other biblical text generally quoted in support of the later developed theory of the double standard, appears hardly to have been used in this way by these early writers at all.[1] Thirdly, the biblical tradition of I Corinthians was no mere afterthought called in to reinforce a double standard theory already accepted on other grounds. On occasions at least it appears as the compelling force driving the Christian interpreter reluctantly in that direction. Thus Clement indignantly asserts the equal value of marriage as compared with celibacy in spite of what he clearly sees to be the most natural rendering of I Cor. vii. 32–3.[2] This element of reluctance gradually diminishes in the majority of subsequent writers. Origen, when interpreting Paul's words about circumcision in I Cor. vii. 20 spiritually with reference to marriage, does claim that fundamentally the choice between marriage and celibacy is a matter of indifference, but the way in which he makes the claim clearly reveals that he really regards himself as making a somewhat generous concession to the married.[3] Far more often he is quite explicit about the superior nature of the unmarried state. Marriage and celibacy are gifts of the same God, but, while marriage is simply a gift, celibacy is a spiritual gift, for no spiritual gift could be a hindrance to prayer as Paul says marriage can be.[4] Marriage is the way of the unprofitable servant who does only what it is his duty to do, celibacy is the way of the good and faithful servant who goes beyond the realm of precept and of duty.[5] Methodius goes still further. Paul, he declares, does not set forth marriage as a command and celibacy as a counsel; it is the other way round; celibacy is the command and marriage a concession allowed only to the sexually uncontrolled.[6] By the time of Chrysostom

---

[1] Note the absence of the idea from Clement of Alexandria's *Quis Dives Salvetur* and from the discussion of the incident in Irenaeus, *Adv. Haer.* 4, 12, 5 (Harvey, II, 179–80). The idea does occur in Origen when he deals with the story in the course of his commentary (*Comm. in Matt.* 15, 12–18), but even there it is not as explicit as might have been expected.

[2] Clement, *Stromateis*, 3, 88, 2–3.

[3] Origen, Frag. on I Cor. vii. 20 (*J.T.S.* IX, 507).

[4] Frag. on I Cor. vii. 7 (*J.T.S.* IX, 503); on Rom. i. 11 (*J.T.S.* XIII, 213–14; *Comm. in Rom.* 1, 12—857B–D).

[5] Origen, *Comm. in Rom.* 3, 3 (933D) on Rom. iii. 12.

[6] Methodius, *Symposium*, 3, 12 (I Cor. vii. 6).

the whole idea of the two standards is fully established and we find it firmly embedded in his sober and careful exegesis. It is still in I Corinthians that he finds the concept most clearly expressed, and in his introductory comments to ch. vii he distinguishes 'that which is good and far more excellent' (τὸ καλὸν καὶ σφόδρα ὑπερέχον) on the one hand from 'that which is safe and suited to assist your weakness' (τὸ ἀσφαλὲς καὶ βοηθοῦν σου τῇ ἀσθενείᾳ) on the other.[1]

As Tertullian had pointed out, it was because of the poverty and immaturity of the Corinthians' faith that a lower standard is set out in the epistle to them.[2] The idea that apparent conflicts or differences in Paul's teaching in different epistles are to be explained in terms of the varying standards of faith and life in the different churches is widely used in the course of exegesis. Jerome explains not only the higher teaching about marriage in Ephesians as compared with Corinthians in this way, but also the fact that the Ephesians are called upon directly to imitate God while the Corinthians are summoned only to the lower standard of an imitation of Paul.[3] Pelagius interprets I Thess. iv. 4 as a call to complete chastity going beyond what was required of the weaker Corinthians.[4] Chrysostom explains the fact that in Romans Paul appears to regard special fast days as a matter of indifference, while in Colossians and Galatians he takes a stronger line on the same issue, as determined by the comparative newness of the Roman Christians' faith.[5] Isidore similarly postulates a very immature faith on the part of the Roman Christians to account for the fact that Paul's injunction to them in Rom. xii. 20 falls short of the full New Testament standard of loving one's enemies; a lower Old Testament standard is given because of the nature of the recipients of the letter.[6]

Chrysostom gives clear expression to this difference of standards

---

[1] Chr. *Hom. in I Cor.* 19, 1 (10, 151) on I Cor. vii. 1; *ibid.* 22, 2 (10, 182–3) on I Cor. ix. 16–18.

[2] See p. 128 above.

[3] Jerome on Eph. v. 24 (531 C, D); on Eph. v. 1 (518 B, C).

[4] Pelagius on I Thess. iv. 4 (p. 429).

[5] Chr. *Hom. in Rom.* 25, 2 (9, 630) on Rom. xiv. 5.

[6] Isidore, *Epp.* 4, 11. Cf. Clement, *Stromateis*, 3, 82, 4, according to which second marriage represents the Old Testament standard and is therefore allowable to the weak although falling short of the full gospel ethic.

with the help of the concept of περισσεία (superabundance). If the Christian has been made free from the law, it is that he may pass beyond it, not that he may transgress it.[1] When Paul prays that the Thessalonians may abound more and more, he is praying that they will not stay only at the realm of obedience to rules.[2] Αὐτάρκεια (sufficiency) may serve for the σαρκικοί but περισσεία is the characteristic of the πνευματικοί.[3]

But the most interesting feature of Chrysostom's interpretation of Paul's moral teaching is his clear recognition of its position in the pattern of Paul's thought as a whole. He draws attention to the normal but by no means rigid or invariable structure of the epistles, according to which there is a doctrinal section followed by a moral one.[4] But more important than the recognition of this distinction is the recognition of the close connection between the two. It is Paul's custom to base his moral exhortation on divine facts.[5] This indeed is the essential differentia between Christian and Greek moral teaching.[6] Humility is the root of all virtue, and for the Christian the root of humility lies in the recollection of the fact and the extent of his salvation.[7] Behind the moral precepts of ordinary Christian living lies the wonder of divine grace.

[1] Chr. *Comm. in Gal.* 5, 4 (10, 669–70) on Gal. v. 13. Chrysostom points out that both the harlot and the virgin have gone outside the bounds of the law but in very different senses. Cf. Eusebius of Emesa on Gal. ii. 18 (Staab, p. 48).

[2] Chr. *Hom. in I Thess.* 5, 1 (11, 423) on I Thess. iv. 1.

[3] Chr. *Hom. in II Cor.* 19, 3 (10, 533) on II Cor. ix. 8.

[4] Chr. *Hom. in I Cor.* 43, 1 (10, 367) on I Cor. xvi. 1; *Comm. in Gal.* 5, 4 (10, 669) on Gal. v. 13.

[5] Chr. *Hom. in Eph.* 10, 1 (11, 75) on Eph. iv. 4 (Eph. v. 2; Phil. ii. 5–6). Cf. Theod. on Rom. xiv. 7–9, where he points out that Paul's moral teaching on the question of eating is based not solely on the idea of creation but also on that of Christ's death for us (Staab, pp. 164–5).

[6] Chr. *Hom. in I Cor.* 18, 2 (10, 147) on I Cor. vi. 20.

[7] Chr. *Hom. in Eph.* 9, 2 (11, 71–2) on Eph. iv. 2.

EPILOGUE

AN ASSESSMENT

We have come to the end of our study and the question that immediately arises in our minds is the question 'How far then did the early commentators give a true interpretation of Paul's meaning?' Yet the very form in which the question arises is not without danger. It implies the assumption that we have a true interpretation of Paul's meaning—or at least a truer one than that of those whom we have studied—in the light of which theirs may be tested and judged. It may be so; but we as much as they are children of our own times and there may well be aspects of Pauline thought to which we are blinded by the particular presuppositions and patterns of theological thinking in our own day. If therefore we seek to pass judgement on other interpreters it can only be in the recognition that we also stand in need of judgement, even and perhaps especially when we are least conscious of that need.

Certainly the early commentators were much influenced by the tendencies of their times. In Pauline thought about the flesh and about the law there appears to be an element of unresolved tension. Gnostic thought, especially in its most Christian form in the teaching of Marcion, had stressed exclusively the element of Paul's hostility in both cases to a degree that was certainly false and equally certainly dangerous. It was inevitable that in orthodox exegesis the pendulum should swing strongly in the opposite direction. As a result, although for the most part they show a sound understanding of these aspects of Paul's thought, the orthodox commentators are apt to be unbalanced and one-sided in their judgements. Thus on the subject of the flesh they are in general right to insist on the moral rather than the physical meaning of the word σάρξ in many Pauline contexts. But in their determination not to deviate an inch from this basic understanding they are inclined to oversimplify the pattern of Paul's thought at the cost of complicating the exegesis of his words. It is somewhat ironic that Origen should have been most bitterly condemned for his teaching on the resurrection body, a point on which he was probably nearer to Paul's thought than his calumniators. So it was also with the concept of the law. The early commentators were right in seeing that Marcion had misunderstood Paul's view of the matter; Paul did see his teaching as a confirmation of the law. But on this issue also they were determined to make Paul entirely self-consistent and thus overemphasized the positive nature of his attitude to the law. But it was not only with himself that Paul had to be shown to be wholly consistent. Their view of inspiration involved the belief that all Scripture was self-consistent in the same thoroughgoing way. Augustine indeed declares that the thing which held him back from accepting and appreciating the value of Paul's writings in the time before his conversion was the way in which they appeared to him to be both self-contradictory and inconsistent with the Old Testament.[1] Thus any exegetical device, however far-fetched, which could remove all trace of apparent internal inconsistency or conflict with the Old Testament was to be welcomed. Two main approaches to the problem predominate in their writings. In the first instance they give great prominence to the educative function of the law as a schoolmaster preparing men for the coming of Christ. In so doing a genuinely Pauline concept is given a proportionately greater emphasis than it holds in the writings of Paul himself, but no serious distortion of his thought would seem to be involved. Secondly, a clear distinction is drawn between the moral and the ceremonial laws. In this case they would seem to be introducing a wholly new line of thought not grounded at all in the writings of Paul himself. Such changes of emphasis and importation of new ideas were the more easily made because the commentators were thinking all the time primarily in terms of their own situation. In the closing years of the fourth century, when most of the commentaries were being written, the problem of the Jewish law was not a pressing issue. They could safely speak in positive terms of its confirmation in Christ without any fear that the Christians who heard them would even for a moment consider that they might be expected to follow it out in every detail. If Jewish critics did press the point, emphasis could always be laid upon the fact that the fulfilment of the law in Christ was of a spiritual nature. It is only

---

[1] Augustine, *Confessiones*, 7, XXI, 27.

very rarely that they make any attempt to enter into the very different conditions of Paul's own day and seek to understand his attitude to the law in the light of his own real situation. For them, living in the midst of a rapidly decaying civilization, the maintenance of law was an issue of the utmost importance. Too often it was in the light of this context that they reflected upon Paul's teaching on the law.

In the realm of Christology also it is the situation of the commentators' day rather than that of Paul's day which dominates the scene. This does not seem to have resulted in any serious distortion of the general substance of Paul's teaching, but it did lead to the introduction of an entirely alien element of precision into their interpretation of Paul's language about the person of Christ. In other words they were right in seeing that Paul's conception of Christ was better understood in terms of Nicene orthodoxy and of that developing line of thought which led ultimately to Chalcedon than in terms of any other rival definition of his person; they were altogether unjustified in seeing the details of those later beliefs explicitly indicated by the specific wording of the Pauline statements.

When we turn on to the great issues of grace, faith and works, we turn to a field in which the early commentators were not so dominated by the exigencies of contemporary debate. It is true that Gnostic determinism was something to be denounced at every opportunity, but the great debate about grace within the Christian Church lay still just in the future. The commentaries of Augustine and of Pelagius both date from before the outbreak of the Pelagian controversy. In this respect it is the modern interpreter who is the more likely to be unduly influenced by the theological situation in which he stands. If the early commentators could only see Paul's teaching about the law through anti-Marcionite spectacles, the majority of Protestant critics of the Fathers have only been able to see their teaching through Reformed and Lutheran spectacles. 'In toto Origene non est verbum unum de Christo', wrote Luther;[1] what no doubt he really meant was that Origen did not teach the

---

[1] Quoted by E. Molland, *The Conception of the Gospel in Alexandrian Theology*, p. 170 n. 2. Molland in an excellent discussion on pp. 170–2 shows how Origen can expound justification very adequately in his Commentary on Romans although the idea is never central to his thought. His thinking is set in a broader cosmic frame than the more narrowly soteriological thinking of Luther.

same doctrine of justification by faith alone which he found in the writings of Paul. That is what many later Protestant writers have really meant when they have complained of the unpauline character of Origen and other patristic writers.[1] In so far as that is what they really wanted to assert, they are undoubtedly correct; but it does not warrant the utter dismissal of the early commentators as totally insensitive to Paul's teaching. The Eastern writers were by no means unconcerned with the concept of divine grace. They fully recognized its prominent position in the teaching of Paul. But they also recognized (and here their fear of any form of Gnostic determinism certainly played its part) that the idea of divine grace must be linked closely with the correlative idea of the freedom of human response. Paul, they argued, was not a systematic theologian, and it was the religious purpose of his writing which led to the apparently one-sided stress on divine grace in his teaching. Once again therefore they endeavoured, however tortuous the detail of the exegesis might prove to be, to present Paul's thought as uniform throughout and as revealing a proper balance between divine grace and human freedom. Yet, while insisting in this way that any systematic exposition of Paul's thought must allow for the free human response of faith, they did not even so regard that faith as being itself a purely human matter. It too was in some important way the gift of God. Yet it could not, they argued, be simply and solely the gift of God, or else there would be nothing to prevent the immediate salvation of all. In the initial act of faith the element of human freedom must be retained. If it be objected that thereby they do make man in the last analysis determinative of his own salvation, two comments may be made. In the first place this type of approach was, with important differences of detailed application, characteristic of all the early commentators, even of Augustine in his early days. As long as the discussion is kept in the terms in which it was then conceived, it is difficult to find any alternative pattern of interpretation short of an unqualified predestinarianism, as the development of Augustine's

---

[1] Cf. M. Werner's judgement of E. Aleith's *Paulus-Verständnis in der alten Kirche*: 'Dieses Buch geht in der Behandlung des Themas noch von einer Interpretation des Paulinismus aus, die mehr an Luthers Lehre als am wirklichen Paulinismus orientiert ist' (quoted by K. Schelkle, *Paulus Lehrer der Väter*, p. 440 n. 1).

thought bears witness. If Augustine's later thought seems to do better justice to some aspects of Paul's teaching, there are other aspects which it reduces to meaninglessness. Secondly, the early writers kept a firm hold on the conception of man as created by God's grace in his image. That which makes the initial response of faith in man is after all not man as over against God but the image of God in man.[1] By that stress they sought to alleviate the apparently irreconcilable conflict between the ideas of divine grace and human freedom.

It would appear to be more in their understanding of the nature of faith than in their accounts of its relation to divine grace that the commentators are apt to misrepresent the substance of Paul's thought. If the Epistle of James was intended as a corrective to certain misunderstandings of Paul's teaching in an antinomian direction, then it certainly performed its task effectively. The great majority of the Fathers see the Pauline conception of faith through the eyes of the author of the Epistle of James. Faith is primarily intellectual assent to certain dogmatic truths; and once that definition of faith has been given it is inevitable that any genuinely religious mind will add on works also as being necessary to salvation. This occurs frequently in the commentaries. Two exceptions to this understanding of the idea of faith are to be found in the earliest of the Greek and of the Latin commentators. Origen puts forward a profound resolution of the whole issue of faith and works in his insistence upon Christ not merely possessing but being his attributes of truth, righteousness, wisdom, peace and so forth. Victorinus in a different way lays a notable emphasis on faith as full personal fellowship and identification with Christ. But the determinative pattern of interpretation in the great majority of the commentaries is closer to that of the Epistle of James than to that of Paul himself.

Two other characteristics of the interpretation of this aspect of Paul's teaching are deserving of note. The concept of merit plays its part in the thought of all the interpreters, even of Augustine in the later stages of his career. Romans ii was felt to show its fully Pauline character as a category for understanding God's dealings with men. It was claimed, not only by Augustine but also by the

[1] Cf. H. Crouzel, *Théologie*, p. 245.

Eastern writers, to be fully consonant with the Pauline teaching about grace if applied only to good works subsequent to faith. The second feature to be noted is the eschatological emphasis in Theodore of Mopsuestia's understanding of Paul's theology. It may be objected that Theodore is false to Paul in stressing death rather than sin as the root of man's problem. But at least it enables him in his presentation of the positive aspects of Paul's thought to declare Paul's message with striking effect as a message of resurrection life experienced in anticipation now and soon to be realized in all its fullness. Theodore has always been noted for the shrewd and careful nature of his comments on the grammatical form and contextual structure of the Epistles. There are certainly times when he forces his own theological system out of the text, but there are also times when his eschatological emphasis leads to a unique insight into Paul's meaning. For example it enables him to appreciate the radical nature of Paul's approach to the question of the law with an unusual degree of penetration. All in all there is a dynamic quality about the commentaries of Theodore which is lacking in the work of many of the other commentators.[1]

The traditional Protestant complaint that the early commentators as a whole present a falsely moralistic understanding of Paul's thought is not without foundation. This moralistic emphasis had already come to characterize Christian thought and writing long before the task of Pauline exegesis had been begun. The experience of Christian missions in different parts of the world has consistently revealed the moralistic tendency of second- and third-generation Christian churches. When the first flush of the preaching of the gospel is over, the predominant task of the Church appears as the bringing up of a new generation in distinctively Christian ways over against the non-Christian traditions of their environment. New converts too need to be taught the agreed patterns of conduct expected of members of the Christian community. These tasks are essential and they are not easily performed without the development of required codes of behaviour of a moralistic, and even of a legalistic, kind. The practice develops first; the rationalizing theological

[1] C. H. Turner ('Greek Patristic Commentaries', p. 512) stresses somewhat one-sidedly Theodore's shortcomings as an interpreter of Paul's theology.

explanation comes later. Processes of this kind were clearly at work in the Church of the second century. Paul had differentiated the Christian way of the obedience of faith from the Jewish way of observance of the law. The *Didache* is equally anxious to differentiate between the ways of Christianity and of Judaism, but does so in a manner which is far more superficial but which is also easier both to inculcate and to practise; the Christian is to fast on the fourth and sixth days of the week in contrast to the Jewish fasts on the second and the fifth.[1] Moreover, if a set pattern of conduct throughout a long period of catechumenate is required before admission to baptism is granted, it is no long step to regarding that conduct as contributing to the attainment of salvation. In their very different ways both the persecutions of the third century and the influx of nominal Christians in the fourth served to enhance this emphasis upon the observance of a set pattern of behaviour. It is hardly surprising if in such a situation the commentators on Paul's epistles should emphasize both the positive aspect of Paul's attitude to the law and the necessity of works. The pattern of church life within which they lived and worked could not but affect their exegesis of Paul's thought in this way. Yet it never made them wholly blind to his message. The priority of divine grace was more widely and more strongly upheld than has often been recognized. Moreover, as we have just seen, an understanding of faith in terms of personal communion with Christ is a prominent feature in the thought both of Origen and of Victorinus. It is perhaps not without significance that both writers were men much influenced by the spiritual character of Middle Platonist and Neoplatonist teaching. It is common to speak of Platonism in relation to the early Church's understanding of the faith of the Bible as being the siren voice which drew men away from the dynamic patterns of biblical thought. But that is certainly not the whole story of the influence it exerted. Neoplatonism was never a popular movement in the sense in which Christianity was. It was therefore in less danger of losing its spiritual quality in a merely moralistic interpretation of man's need. It may have helped to keep alive amongst Christian thinkers a more spiritual approach to the message of Paul, and it would appear at least to have been

[1] *Didache*, 8.

one important factor in opening the eyes of Augustine to the truth and profundity of that message.

No brief or simple answer can be given to the question how far the early commentators truly understood the mind of Paul. The early exegetical tradition is often forced in its detailed outworking, but there is more in it which reveals than which distorts the text which it expounds. Nevertheless, the total impression which it leaves upon the reader is that Paul has been tamed in the process. In part that is inevitable. A work of commentary can never have the same dynamic vitality as the original which it sets out to interpret. In this instance this general tendency was exaggerated by two main causes. In the first place Paul's interpreters were writing for the everyday needs of a Church whose nature as an established community and whose situation within the Roman Empire were totally different from what they had been in Paul's day. In the second place their understanding of Scripture required that Paul's vigorous affirmations be reduced to a wholly self-consistent system. For all their recognition of the pragmatic, religious intention of his letters, they still felt the need to show that all his words were true as general philosophical statements about the precise nature of God and man. Thus pedagogic utility and philosophical systematization were always important aspects of their aim in the work of commentary. Such aims are likely to tame the writings of the most vigorous prophet.

There is no single commentator of whom we may assert that he catches and reflects the fullness of Paul's thought. If Chrysostom's commentaries are the most consistently sound and reliable in their judgements, they yet lack conspicuously that penetration of sympathetic insight which alone could fully justify the panegyrics which some later writers have heaped upon them. On the other hand, there is no commentator whose work has come down to us in any quantity in whose writings there are not to be found comments of real and lasting worth. For all their very real shortcomings, at least the theory that the thought of Paul was totally lost in the obscurity of a dark Pelagian world until the shining of the great Augustinian light is one deserving to be dismissed to that very limbo of outworn ideas in which it would itself seek to place the early patristic commentaries on the writings of the divine apostle.

BIBLIOGRAPHY

A. PRIMARY SOURCES: ANCIENT COMMENTARIES ON
THE PAULINE EPISTLES

(1) *Greek*

Origen, Commentary on Romans (translated by Rufinus) (*P.G.* 14, 833–1292).
Commentary on Romans iii. 5–v. 7 (Greek text), ed. J. Scherer, Cairo, 1957.
Fragments on Romans (ed. H. Rambsbotham), *J.T.S.* XIII (1912), 210–24,
357–68 and *J.T.S.* XIV (1913), 10–22.
Fragments on I Corinthians (ed. C. Jenkins), *J.T.S.* IX (1908), 232–47,
353–72, 500–14, and *J.T.S.* X (1909), 29–51.
Fragments on Ephesians (ed. J. A. F. Gregg), *J.T.S.* III (1902), 234–44,
398–420, and 554–76.
John Chrysostom, Commentary on Galatians and Homilies on all the other
Pauline Epistles (*P.G.* 60–2).
Theodore of Mopsuestia, Commentaries on the Minor Epistles of St Paul, ed.
H. B. Swete (2 vols.), Cambridge, 1880–2.
Cyril of Alexandria, Fragments on Romans, I and II Corinthians, ed. P. E. Pusey,
Oxford, 1872. (Volume III of Pusey's edition of Cyril's Commentary on
St John's Gospel, pp. 173–361.)
K. Staab, *Pauluskommentare aus der griechischen Kirche* (Neutestamentliche
Abhandlungen, XV), Münster, 1933. (For fragments from the writings of
Didymus, Eusebius of Emesa, Acacius of Caesarea, Apollinarius, Diodore,
Theodore of Mopsuestia and Severian of Gabala.)
J. A. Cramer, *Catenae in Sancti Pauli Epistolas* (3 vols.), Oxford, 1841–4. (For
fragments from the writings of Methodius.)

(2) *Latin*

Victorinus, Commentaries on Galatians, Philippians and Ephesians (*P.L.* 8,
1145–1294).
Ambrosiaster, Commentaries on all the Pauline Epistles (*P.L.* 17, 45–462 and
503–8).
Jerome, Commentaries on Galatians, Ephesians and Philemon (*P.L.* 26, 307–554
and 599–618).
Augustine, Exposition of certain statements from the Epistle to the Romans,
Incomplete commentary on Romans, and Commentary on Galatians
(*P.L.* 35, 2063–2148).
Pelagius, Expositions of the Thirteen Epistles of St Paul, ed. A. Souter, Cam-
bridge, 1922.

Page references to these editions are given in brackets in the notes. The three
volumes of Chrysostom's Homilies are volumes 9, 10 and 11 of the Migne
edition of Chrysostom's works and are distinguished by the use of those num-
bers before the page reference.

BIBLIOGRAPHY

B. SECONDARY SOURCES: PRINCIPAL MODERN WORKS
CONSULTED AND CITED IN THE TEXT

E. Aleith, *Das Paulus-Verständnis in der alten Kirche*, Berlin, 1937.

B. Altaner, *Patrologie* (6th ed.), Freiburg, 1963 (E.T. of 5th edition by H. C. Graef, Edinburgh–London, 1960).

F. Barth, 'Tertullians Auffassung des Apostels Paulus und seines Verhältnisses zu den Uraposteln', *Jahrbücher für Protestantische Theologie* (1882), pp. 706–56.

E. Benz, 'Das Paulus-Verständnis in der morgenländischen und abendländischen Kirche', *Z.R.G.* III (1951), 289–309.

C. Bigg, *Christian Platonists of Alexandria*, Oxford, 1913.

E. C. Blackman, *Marcion and his Influence*, London, 1948.

F. Buri, *Clemens Alexandrinus und der paulinische Freiheitsbegriff*, Zurich, 1939.

J. Burnaby, *Amor Dei*, London, 1960.

G. W. Butterworth, *Origen on First Principles*, London, 1936.

H. Chadwick, 'Eucharist and Christology in the Nestorian Controversy', *J.T.S.* n.s. II (1951), 145–64.

—— 'Origen, Celsus and the Stoa', *H.T.R.* XLI (1948), 83–102.

—— 'Rufinus and the Tura Papyrus of Origen's Commentary on Romans', *J.T.S.* n.s. X (1959), 10–42.

W. O. Chadwick, *John Cassian*, Cambridge, 1950.

F. H. Chase, *Chrysostom, a study in the history of Biblical Interpretation*, Cambridge, 1887.

H. Crouzel, *Théologie de l'image de Dieu chez Origène*, Paris, 1956.

J. Daniélou, *Origène*, Paris, 1948 (E.T. by W. Mitchell, London and New York, 1955).

W. D. Davies, *Paul and Rabbinic Judaism*, London, 1955.

R. Deveréesse, 'Chaînes exégétiques grecques', *Dictionnaire de la Bible*, Supplément I, pp. 1083–1234.

C. H. Dodd, 'ΕΝΝΟΜΟΣ ΧΡΙΣΤΟΥ', in *Studia Paulina in Honorem J. de Zwaan*, Haarlem, 1953.

B. Drewery, *Origen and the Doctrine of Grace*, London, 1960.

R. M. Grant, *The Letter and the Spirit*, London, 1957.

—— 'Tatian and the Bible', in *Studia Patristica*, I (ed. K. Aland and F. L. Cross), pp. 297–306.

H. M. Gwatkin, *Studies of Arianism* (2nd ed.), Cambridge, 1900.

R. P. C. Hanson, *Allegory and Event*, London, 1959.

M. Harl, *Origène et la fonction révélatrice du Verbe Incarné*, Paris, 1958.

A. Harnack, *Der kirchengeschichtliche Ertrag der exegetischen Arbeiten des Origenes*, Leipzig, 1919.

E. Hoffman-Aleith, 'Das Paulus-Verständnis des Johannes Chrysostomus', *Z.N.W.* XXXVIII (1939), 181–8.

G. W. H. Lampe, *The Seal of the Spirit*, London, 1951.

J. Lawson, *Biblical Theology of St Irenaeus*, London, 1948.

J. B. Lightfoot, *Epistle of St Paul to the Galatians*, London, 1890.

—— *Epistle of St Paul to the Philippians*, London, 1890.

—— *Epistles of St Paul to the Colossians and to Philemon*, London, 1890.

H. de Lubac, *Histoire et Esprit: l'intelligence de l'Écriture d'après Origène*, Paris, 1950.

A. Merzagora, 'Giovanni Crisostomo, Commentatore di S. Paolo', *Didaskaleion*, n.s. X (1931), 1, pp. 1–73.

E. Molland, *The Conception of the Gospel in Alexandrian Theology*, Oslo, 1938.

J. Y. Mullins, 'Paul's Thorn in the Flesh', *J.B.L.* LXXVI, pt iv (Dec. 1957), 299–303.

J. Munck, *Paulus und die Heilsgeschichte*, Copenhagen, 1954 (E.T. by F. Clarke, London, 1959).

R. A. Norris, *Manhood and Christ*, Oxford, 1963.

G. Nygren, 'The Augustinian Conception of Grace', in *Studia Patristica*, II (ed. K. Aland and F. L. Cross), pp. 258–69.

W. Sanday and A. C. Headlam, *The Epistle to the Romans* (2nd ed.), Edinburgh, 1896.

J. N. Sanders, review of K. H. Schelkle, *Paulus Lehrer der Väter*, *J.T.S.*n.s. VIII (1957), 315–16.

K. H. Schelkle, *Paulus Lehrer der Väter*, Düsseldorf, 1936.

H. J. Schoeps, *Paulus*, Tübingen, 1959 (E.T. by H. Knight, London, 1961).

H. Seeseman, 'Das Paulusverständnis des Clemens Alexandrinus', *Theologische Studien und Kritiken*, CVII (1936), 312–46.

M. Simon, *Verus Israel*, Paris, 1948.

A. Souter, *The Earliest Latin Commentaries on the Epistles of St Paul*, Oxford, 1927.

—— *A Study of Ambrosiaster*, Cambridge, 1905.

R. E. Taylor, 'Attitudes of the Fathers towards the Practices of Jewish Christians', in *Studia Patristica*, IV (ed. F. L. Cross), pp. 504–11.

C. H. Turner, 'Greek Patristic Commentaries on the Pauline Epistles', Hastings, *Dictionary of the Bible*, extra volume, pp. 484–531.

H. E. W. Turner, *The Patristic Doctrine of Redemption*, London, 1952.

—— *The Pattern of Christian Truth*, London, 1954.

W. Volker, 'Paulus bei Origenes', *Theologische Studien und Kritiken*, CII (1930), 258–79.

J. Werner, *Der Paulinismus des Irenaeus*, Leipzig, 1889.

M. Werner, *Die Entstehung des christlichen Dogmas problemgeschichtlich dargestellt*, Tübingen, 1954 (E.T. by S. G. F. Brandon, London, 1957).

U. Wickert, 'Die Persönlichkeit des Paulus in den Paulus-Kommentaren Theodors von Mopsuestia', *Z.N.W.* LIII (1962), 51–66.

—— *Studien zu den Pauluskommentaren Theodors von Mopsuestia*, Berlin, 1962.

M. F. Wiles, *The Spiritual Gospel*, Cambridge, 1960.

INDEX OF PROPER NAMES

INDEX OF TEXTS

(a) BIBLICAL

(*b*) PATRISTIC

In this index only those authors whose works have been most frequently quoted are included; authors whose works have been less extensively used are included in the index of proper names.

CHRYSOSTOM (*cont.*)

13, 4	27
13, 5–6	124
13, 6	40
13, 7	40, 41, 124
13, 7–8	43
13, 8	45, 46, 125
14, 2	124
14, 3	36, 40
14, 4	126
14, 6	41, 126
14, 7	23
15, 1	95
15, 3	87
16, 2	100
16, 5–6	95
16, 6	124
16, 9	96
17, 1	64
17, 2	123
19, 1	97
19, 5	96
25, 2	130
26, 3	106
29, 2	124

Homilies on I Corinthians

4, 1	123
6, 1	23
7, 4	40
9, 3	125
12, 2	107
15, 2	19, 40
18, 2	131
18, 3	43
19, 1	130
20, 3	85
22, 2	130
23, 1–2	42, 124
23, 2	124
26, 2	87
29, 3	93, 106
38, 5	23
39, 3	45
39, 4	82
39, 5	90
41, 2	46
41, 3	45, 46
42, 1	29

CHRYSOSTOM (*cont.*)

42, 2	57
43, 1	131

Homilies on II Corinthians

1, 3	23
2, 1	124
2, 2–3	23
6, 2	63
7, 1	56
8, 2	97
8, 3	23
10, 1	45
10, 3	45
14, 2	18
16, 2	18
19, 3	131
21, 1	18
26, 2	23
30, 2	93

Commentary on Galatians

1, 7	14
1, 11	23
2, 1	22
2, 2	70
2, 4	22
2, 7	57
2, 8	125
3, 5	88
4, 2	125
5, 2–3	70
5, 4	131
5, 6	27, 63, 107
6, 3	16

Homilies on Ephesians

1, 1	86
1, 2	96, 108, 124
1, 4	88
2, 1	95
2, 2	126
4, 3	124
5, 2	124
5, 4	40
9, 2	131
10, 1	131
11, 3	17
13, 2	125
19, 2	108
24, 2	123